Sell Yourself!

501 Ways to Get Them to Buy From YOU

America's No. 1 Self-Promotion Resource for Sales Professionals!

With brief contributions from:
Anthony Robbins – *Unlimited Power*
Brian Tracy – *The Psychology of Selling*
Zig Ziglar – *See You at the Top*

Fred Berns

Praise for

Sell Yourself!

"*Sell Yourself!* is a veritable plum pudding of resourceful and penny-wise techniques on how to promote yourself successfully. The book is full of great tips from ways to use business cards and stationery for self-promotion to how to implement a million-dollar self-promotion program on a shoestring budget. It will be a source of inspiration for readers who know that you need to do more than make a good first impression. That isn't enough. This book shows you how to make a lasting impression."

> —Michael Michalko, author, *Thinkertoys*
> *(A Handbook of Business Creativity)*
> and *Cracking Creativity (The Secrets of*
> *Creative Geniuses)*

"*Sell Yourself* should be required reading for all entrepreneurs. This book is packed with hands-on techniques for making a business memorable."

> —Jerry Ann Jinnett, author, *Anatomy of a*
> *Business Plan* and *Target Marketing*

"This is one of the best books I have read when it comes to self-promotion. The action items alone are worth much more than the price of the book. If you want to sell yourself and grow your business, just follow the recommendations in Fred's book."

> —Richard Gerson, PhD, author,
> *Marketing Strategies for Small Businesses*

"You can't lose with 501 separate ideas to promote yourself—and that's in addition to ten savvy chapters. All of us have to become good self-promoters if we want to get ahead at anything we do. It works for me; it will work for you."

> —Bob Nelson, author,
> *1001 Ways to Reward Employees* and
> *Consulting for Dummies*

"Simple direct, and extremely relevant to anyone selling himself or his company's offerings. Berns has done an excellent job in communicating the 'what,' 'why,' and 'how' of selling yourself. He tells the reader what is important, why it is important, and how to do it."
— Rich George, author, *Delight Me:*
The 10 Commandments of Customer Service

"This book captures the impossible-to-find strategies necessary for personal sales success. Anyone trying to sell without reading this book is attempting to succeed with their eyes closed!"
— Jerry R. Wilson, CSP, professional speaker,
author *Word-of-Mouth Marketing*

"Behind this cover are the step-by-step rules of personal selling. Whatever your career is, you must be a master at personal selling. Read these rules; use them!"
— Anthony Parinello, author,
The Power of Will and *Selling to VITO*

"Fred has given the sales profession an insightful fresh look at the sales process. Interesting and must reading for serious sales professionals or new sales reps."
— Tim Connor, speaker and trainer, author,
Best Selling, Soft Sell

"This book is full of solid, dependable marketing advice. If you're eager to grow your business, you'll find yourself highlighting something on just about every page!"
— Marcia Yudkin, author,
Six Steps to Free Publicity

"Fred Berns understands the need for salespeople and self-employed consultants to put their best selves forward in today's noisy, competitive marketplace."
— Ron Zemke, author,
Delivering Knock Your Socks Off Service

"Tons of specific ideas you can put to use. Fred not only shows you how, but helps you to get out there and do it!"
— Rick Crandall, PhD, author,
1001 Ways to Market Your Services

Sell Yourself!

501 Ways to Get Them to Buy From YOU

Joan

Best of [...] [...] [...]

Your [...] [...].

[signature]

Sell Yourself!

501 Ways to Get Them to Buy From YOU

Fred Berns

Select Press
Corte Madera, CA

Fred Berns
Power Promotion, Inc.
394 Rendezvous Dr.
Lafayette, CO 80026
303-665-6688

Sell Yourself! 501 Ways to Get Them to Buy
from YOU/ Fred Berns

ISBN 1-890-777-01-3

Printed in the United States of America
10 9 8 7 6 5 4 3 2

*Dedicated with love to
four people to whom it was
never necessary for me
to sell myself:
Mom, Dad, Ellen,
and Zachary*

Contents

INTRODUCTION

Let me introduce you...to you.

You're good at what you do, and you're committed to becoming better. You wouldn't have picked up this book if you weren't.

But chances are you're *not* as good at telling *others* how good you are. It's easier for you to talk about your products than to talk about yourself.

In some ways, you are your own best-kept secret.

The problem with that is that you're not the only one who does what you do or wants what you want. Yours is never the only offer, proposal, recommendation, bid, application, plan, resume, proposition, deal, or sales pitch under consideration by those you seek to influence. That's why you need to stand out from your competitors, accentuate your assets, and promote your positives.

This book is intended to sell you on the idea of selling yourself.

It's a book about selling, and sales professionals are a key, but not the only target audience. *Sell Yourself!* is also designed for entrepreneurs, franchisees, home-based professionals, service providers, and others who are largely responsible for their own marketing.

In a larger sense, it's a book designed for the corporation in which you're a key player: your *personal* corporation.

That's the corporation in which you have many responsibilities. You're the president, the chief executive officer, chairman of the board, and top financial officer. You're the marketing director—and, for that matter, the entire marketing division.

You're about to learn simple strategies that will help you increase your visibility, credibility, competitive position, status, stature, self-esteem, self-confidence, career focus, recognition, and rewards. You'll learn a skill that will determine how far and how fast you advance in your career.

It's a skill they never taught us in school, but should have. Not a day goes by that you don't need it or can't use it. It's a skill practiced by the world's most prominent and prosperous business professionals.

The skill is self-promotion.

If Mission #1 of this book is to sell you on the idea of selling yourself, Mission #2 is to sell you on the idea of selling yourself *differently*. Successful self-promoters dare to be different.

Finally, some thoughts on bragging.

Self-promotion is *not* bragging. It's *selling*. It's accentuating the positive about who you are and what you do.

Why do some sales professionals distinguish between promoting their products and services, and promoting themselves? Why are they so eager to "inform" others of their goods—yet so reluctant to "brag" about themselves.

Dizzy Dean never considered it bragging. Neither should you. Dean, the eminent baseball pitcher and philosopher, was once quoted as saying: "If you done done what you *say* you done done, than saying what you done done ain't bragging."

No, it's not bragging to put yourself in the best possible light. It's just plain old-fashioned, good business sense. No matter what your job description is, has been, or will be, you're a sales person—a personal-sales person. The personal sale is and always will be your most important sale.

Sell Yourself! will help you make that sale.

Fred Berns

CHAPTER ONE

Create Your Commercial

"If you can't succinctly explain how you're special to 'the man or woman on the street,' you're headed for trouble."
—Tom Peters

Y ou can't do the best job of selling your "stuff" until you do the best job of selling yourself.

People don't buy from companies, they buy from people. Those high-tech, state-of-the-art products of yours will sit on a shelf, and your services will be ignored, if you can't make the personal sale. Buyers will take their business elsewhere if you fail to sell them on buying from you.

The sale begins with a "commercial."

Your commercial is the 30-second presentation, the 50-word message that establishes who you are and what you do. It's your time in the spotlight, those fleeting seconds in which you introduce yourself.

How do you spend those defining moments?

Your Personal Commercial

Do you share a meaningful message that others remember? Or is it one that others forget, as they tune it—and you—out?

1

Consider the importance of your message. It's the focal point around which your personal promotion efforts revolve. It's your handle, your label, your principal selling point.

There is magic in your personal message. And—there are problems if you don't have a personal message. With a commercial, you position yourself as one-of-a-kind. Without a commercial, you're a listing in a database, a face in the crowd, a nobody.

Think of your *message* as what it takes to get your prospects' attention, *marketing* as what it takes to get them in your door, and *selling* as what you do after they get there.

Your message—your commercial—establishes your professional identity. It helps you overcome stereotypes prospects might attach to your business. It's human nature for people you meet to generalize and think that people "like you" are quite similar. "Like you" might include persons in your occupation, industry, company, etc. They assume you are the same as others in your field—until you give them reason to assume otherwise.

That reason is your personal commercial.

Your Positioning

Create your commercial by answering a question that you may have first confronted back in grade school. Think back to one of those occasions when you did something you weren't supposed to—talked out of turn, maybe, or left the room without signing out—and the teacher pulled you aside and said: "Young man (lady), just who do you think you *are*?"

Same question now, in a different context: "Who DO you think you are?" What makes you different? Your experience? Your product knowledge? The benefits you provide your customers?

These are dollars-and-cents questions, considering the link between your commercial and the price you get for your services. You can get any fee that you set, providing you can adequately differentiate yourself from those who charge less.

Too many individuals, and the companies they work

for, just don't get it. A survey by the accounting firm of Coopers & Lybrand shows that only half the companies polled consider the uniqueness of their goods and services when they establish their prices.

A sales rep fails to differentiate herself from competitors if she continues to face price resistance from her customers and prospects.

> "Positioning is not what you do to a product. Positioning is what you do to the mind of a prospect."
> —Jack Trout and Al Ries, *Positioning: The Battle for Your Mind*

"Unless a business is clearly differentiated from its competitors in ways that are meaningful to customers, the price issue will be a constant irritant," writes John R. Graham in the newsletter *Executive Edge*.

Designing Your Commercial

Perhaps you don't give your commercial much thought. You should! Your commercial is unique to you. No one else has, or ever will have, your commercial.

There are those inclined to keep their commercials a secret. When they do share their personal messages, they may precede them with comments like:

"Sorry to bother you, but..."
"This may not interest you, but..."
"For what it's worth..."
"I won't take much of your time..."
"Is this a bad time?"

Then there are those so eager to talk about their products and services that they forget to talk about themselves. Their personal commercials fall by the wayside. So does their credibility.

Denied personal messages, their customers may as well shop online or through catalogs.

Include some of the "Victory Vocabulary" words (see box on the next page) in your marketing materials, and you'll describe yourself in ways that others in your field do not.

Why those others do not, I can't understand. Because we're all "unique," we approach our tasks in a "special" and "distinctive" way. We are "skilled" and "knowledgeable" about what we do.

Certainly all of us are "able" and "capable," not to mention "effective" and "efficient" in our professional duties.

Your "Only"

Most people don't even consider those words for their personal commercials. No matter which words you choose to describe yourself, make sure "only" is one of them.

"Only" is far and away the most powerful word in the Victory Vocabulary.

"Only." What a word! It's the word that most distinguishes you from your competitors. It puts you in a class by yourself, highlighting your uniqueness and signaling that you have what others lack.

Identify yourself as the only local manufacturer with a public showroom, the only financial officer with 20 years experience, or the firm's only bilingual attorney, and you set yourself apart.

To say that you're the only account executive in your area who's worked with *Fortune* 500 companies, or the *only* scientist who has probed a rare tropical disease, or the *only* sales representative to lead the company six consecutive months—well, *that's* special.

Your four-color, 50-page, state-of-the-art marketing kit, your glossy,

Victory Vocabulary

Replace your "striving" words with these "arriving" words:

Able	Foremost	Profound
Accomplished	Gifted	Prominent
Acclaimed	Highly-regarded	Proven
Adept	Highest	Qualified
Award-winning	Honored	Rare
Awesome	Impressive	Recognized
Brilliant	Incomparable	Renowned
Capable	Illustrious	Remarkable
Celebrated	Knowledgeable	Saluted
Commendable	Leading	Savvy
Committed	Magnificent	Shrewd
Creative	Marketwise	Singular
Dedicated	Masterful	Skilled
Distinctive	Notable	Special
Effective	Noteworthy	Striking
Efficient	Novel	Successful
Eminent	Often-quoted	Superb
Esteemed	Only	Talented
Excellent	Outstanding	Top-rated
Exceptional	Paramount	Unconventional
Experienced	Phenomenal	Unequaled
Expert	Prestigious	Unique
Extraordinary	Principal	Unparalleled
Famous	Professional	Wise
Formidable	Proficient	Worthy

The Power of "Only"

I discovered the power of "only" months after I set out to establish an independent radio news service in Washington, DC in 1976. My idea was to provide localized news out of the nation's capital for radio stations.

I intended to report on the votes of local Congressmen, cover the testimony at Congressional hearings of visiting local city officials, and produce stories on home-town folks who had relocated in Washington.

Weeks on the road trying to sell radio news directors on the idea of my freelance service yielded few results.

Finally, two stations, KOLT in Scottsbluff, Nebraska and KFIZ in Fond du Lac, Wisconsin, agreed to try out my service. The deal: $5 for every story of mine that they used on the air.

I returned home flush with the feeling of self-importance. I was convinced that once I advertised, other radio station news directors would come running.

They didn't. The costly ads I took out in various broadcasting trade publications yielded nothing. The longer I sat in my new office, the quieter it became. The calls didn't come in. My patience was running out. So was my money.

One morning I attended an entrepreneur's workshop conducted by the Small Business Administration's SCORE staff. The first speaker suggested that we "look around at your neighbors, because two out of three of them will be out of business within 18 months." It wasn't exactly the motivational boost I was seeking.

During a break, a classmate suggested that I send a news release to *Broadcasting* magazine promoting my service as the "only bureau of its kind with clients around the nation."

The only service of its kind...

"Hey, all I do is occasional work for one small station in Wisconsin and a smaller one in Nebraska?" I replied. "I can't promote myself as having "'clients around the nation.'"

"Why not?" he replied. "What do you have to lose?"

A week later I wrote my first press release, a paragraph on my new letterhead stationery, announcing the only independent news service of its kind serving radio stations "around the country." Within days after *Broadcasting* ran the blurb, news directors called seeking more information about this one-of-a-kind news service serving radio stations "around the country."

Six weeks after the blurb appeared, 35 news directors had signed up to use the only service of its kind for stations "around the country."

Several months later, a Toronto radio station called. After that, I started promoting my bureau as the *only* one of its kind serving stations "around the world." Inquiries came in from countries from Australia to West Germany.

By the time I sold the Berns Bureau in April, 1992, it was the only news organization of its kind that over a 16-year period had served more than 5,000 broadcast and print outlets—around the country and around the world.

award-winning brochure, your flashy resume—may impress others. But it's your "only" commercial that they will remember.

Your "only" is what they'll think of first, and what they'll use to judge you and to tell someone else about you.

In the box on the previous page, I recounted my discovery of the power of "only." If *only* I had known, in those early days of struggle, the power of the word "only!"

You, too, should find that power, and do what you can to develop your "only list." The "onlys" will come easier when you consider your experience, the services and products you offer, the area in which you specialize, the clients you serve, your education, and even your hobbies and special interests.

> **⚠ WARNING! Don't Be Modest**
>
> Be advised that the same word that helps you express your uniqueness can also hinder you. "Only" becomes a liability when you use it to mean "merely."
>
> "I'm only a government securities analyst," a woman told me following a workshop. "You can't expect *me* to market myself, can you?"
>
> "Don't tell me you're 'only a securities analyst,'" I responded. "Begin the sentence by telling me you're 'the only securities analyst who _____.'"
>
> Use "only," as she did, to limit others' expectations of you, and the word serves to put you down rather than build you up.

Don't Be Like Everyone Else

You have a chance to make an impact when someone asks you the most basic of all questions: "What do you do?"

So many individuals respond to that question by mumbling their job title and a few words about who they work for. They neglect to mention what others receive as a result of working with them.

Those individuals play the "Same Game" of self-promotion. It's very easy to play: simply promote yourself the same way that your competitors promote themselves. That may mean placing an ad in the Yellow Pages, or launching a direct mail campaign, or relying on word-of-mouth recognition.

The Same Game is a game without winners. It's not so much an exercise in "Follow the Leader" as in "Follow the Follower."

Don't Be a Follower

There can be danger in "following." Consider the fate of processionary caterpillars, which have been known to follow each other around the rim of a flowerpot full of food until they dropped dead of starvation!

Want to attend a Same Game? Stop by a local networking meeting and listen as the participants talk about themselves and their organizations.

Watch how they discuss who they are, who they work for, what their job titles are, and what they do. Notice how no one spells out the unique benefits he or she provides. Notice how few share their unique qualifications and explain how they differ from others in their fields.

Their words could just as easily come out of the mouths of their competitors. They're all talking the same talk.

The Right Commercial

You can rise above the Same Game by adopting a message that brings out the best in you. Your message can demonstrate how you stand out within your profession. How? By focusing on your achievements, skills, or other aspects of your career

Your commercial can build bridges. Use it to create connections with customers previously linked to your predecessors or competitors. Those connections help when customers are favorably impressed by those they worked with before you. In those circumstances, you need to establish your reputation at the same time you try to overcome the reputation of your predecessors. Your mission: Call attention to your commercial and make no references to those of your competitors.

Your commercial can bridge the gap with those who have predisposed notions about your industry, your profession—or you. Others may have negative perceptions that have nothing to do with your performance. Nevertheless, you must do everything you can do to overcome the misperceptions.

Your commercial can help you differentiate yourself from negative stereotypes—especially if you avoid titles or buzzwords that trigger them. If your title (e.g., exterminator, public relations agent) creates problems, use alternatives (e.g., pest management specialist, communications advisor).

> **Wrong Commercials**
>
> Your commercial can work against you if it sends out the wrong signals. You weaken your message, for example, when you attribute your success to luck or when you bad-mouth competitors. **STOP**

One Colorado-based agent for a national financial services firm with a poor reputation found that his business picked up when he deleted the company's name from his marketing materials. His success increased once he began referring to himself as "an estate planning specialist."

Getting Attention

Corporate America thinks enough of commercials to invest millions of dollars in them annually. Fortunately, you don't have to shell out that kind of cash for *your* commercial. But commercials present both you and major corporations with one common challenge: gaining and maintaining attention.

Madison Avenue execs know that many people don't watch or listen to their commercials. Often they turn off the sound, channel surf, or simply leave the room when commercials come on.

You, too, run the risk that people will tune out your commercial. You must cut through the clutter, penetrate their preoccupation, and get your message across. Your commercial shouldn't *sound* like a commercial. And it won't—if you create a concise personal message that focuses on the benefits you provide.

Practice to Be Spontaneous!

It's never easy to deliver a credible commercial, but you'll increase your chances of doing so if you present it, rather than just speak it.

Rehearse it as you would any other major presentation. Practice it repeatedly. Review, revise, and fine tune it until it's smooth and polished—and then practice it some more. Run your commercial by colleagues and trusted advisors, and listen carefully to their feedback.

Videotape yourself rehearsing your commercial. The camera is the best trainer of all.

Practice making eye contact, smiling, and varying your vocal inflection as you communicate your message. Alter your pace. Enunciate with care. Strive for a relaxed, conversational tone. Try pausing for emphasis.

Do all that and your message will come across as heartfelt and sincere. Focus attention on it by not pursuing other activities while you communicate it. Don't pass out your business card while you're talking or do anything else that might divert attention from your message.

You may share your commercial a dozen times in a day, but it shouldn't come across that way. Each presentation must seem like your *first* presentation, each performance must seem like opening night.

Strive to keep your message fresh, and your presentation spontaneous.

Yul Brynner did. After several better-known actors turned down the role, Brynner began playing the King of Siam in 1951 in the Broadway play *The King and I.* Following its three-year run, Brynner played the part in two successful Broadway revivals.

Brynner played the king in a total of 4,625 performances, but theater critics and his audiences never complained that *his* performance was stale.

Train Others to Sell You

How you present your commercial will determine its impact. Unfortunately, you don't always have the opportunity to make that presentation. There are times when you must rely on others to deliver your commercial.

Those others never recreate your enthusiasm and passion about your message. Whether they use your words, or substitute some of their own, something always gets lost in translation.

Leave nothing to chance, and do what you can to insure that your message will stand alone. If others are to relay your message, provide them with a simple written version. Review and rehearse the commercial together.

When you are to be formally introduced—prior to a speech, for example—supply a brief, double-spaced, fully capitalized written introduction. Make it easy for your host, and you'll both be better off.

Your Elevator Speech

One excellent way to create a concise message is to practice what author Lisbeth Wiley Chapman calls the "elevator drill." She describes it as "an exercise that you practice so you can tell someone what you do in the length of time it takes for an elevator door to close."

That can make for a capsulated and effective account. It's best to present your commercial in small doses over time rather than in major helpings.

Think of the last time you visited a bookstore. When a book interested you, did you plop down on the floor and read the entire thing? Or did you gaze at the cover, scan the introduction, and turn a few pages?

Think of your commercial as your "cover," your introduction page, your preview. If others are interested, and certainly they will be, they will probe further to get the rest of your story.

It makes sense, therefore, to prioritize the bits of information you share about yourself. How and who you help might be the first dose of information you release, followed by the products and services you provide, then your job title and employer.

Using Your Commercial

Crafting a powerful personal commercial takes work, but the time you spend on it is an investment in your future. Consider all the ways you'll use that commercial—from individual sales calls to group presentations, from job interviews to media interviews, from networking meetings to social events.

"I'm the only bilingual mortgage banker in my firm."

You can adapt your commercial to fit different audiences and circumstances. Point out in a speech to doctors, for example, how you specialize in helping "physicians and others." Match the benefits you offer to the needs audience members express. Follow your commercial with a soft sell; e.g., "If you're looking to move your office, give me a call."

Make your commercial available to the person who introduces you at a company meeting. Provide it to an editor as a way of introducing your article.

However you use it, it will simplify your personal sale. A good commercial provides consistency, credibility, and pizzazz to the way you present yourself.

A polished personal commercial lessens the likelihood that you'll be at a loss for words when you enter a key meeting or networking event. That entrance can be intimidating. But a powerful personal message can help break the ice, and pull you through it.

Your commercial is a mighty weapon when the risks are high and much is at stake. Consider a face-to-face meeting with a key prospect, or a key decision maker you seek to impress. This is not a time for much original thought. You don't want to grope for words or scramble to recall pertinent facts about yourself. You don't want to start anew each time you present yourself to a person of influence. With a tried, true, and tested personal commercial, you won't have to.

To make an impact with your message, tune into radio stations that those you seek to influence listen to all the time. The call letters of one of those stations is WII-FM. It's the "What's In It For Me?" station, the one people dial to discover if what you say relates to them.

The other station, WMYD, stands for "What Makes You Different?" People turn to that station to find out if they should care about you and what you have to say.

Be a Specialist

One thing that makes you different is the fact that you're a "specialist."

You have special skills, and you apply them in special ways. You have a special area of expertise. You focus your efforts on working with special clients.

To differentiate yourself, identify how and with whom you specialize. Gone are the days when you can

---

Set Yourself Apart with Focus, Perseverance, and Action

The first step to achieving the success of which you are capable is having a clear focus on what you want. You have to believe in yourself and know how to persevere.

Try different things to see what works for you. Educate yourself. Read books, listen to tapes and attend seminars on positive thinking and personal growth. Have an action plan.

You know, I wasn't exactly an overnight success. I started off as a cookware salesman, sold just about everything, and pursued my dream to be a speaker for 16 years before I was able to devote full time to that career. But I always had a goal.

J.C. Penney put it perfectly when he said, "Give me a stock clerk with a goal and I'll give you a man who will make history. Give me a man without a goal, and I'll give you a stock clerk."

One of my favorite sayings, because I've found it to be the truest, is, "You can have everything you want in life if you help enough other people get what they want." Whether your goal is happier customers or happier employees, the philosophy is the same. Find out that they want...and give it to them.

—Zig Ziglar

use a general title (sales rep, author, travel agent) to effectively promote yourself. In this era of increased specialization, you need to identify your special niche.

The easiest way to do that is to carefully examine your client list. No one else serves the same clients in the same way. No one else specializes in helping the same people as you do.

Nor do your competitors have the exact same attributes as you. Compile a list of at least 10 qualities that set you apart from those competitors. Create a dazzling message by including some of those qualities within it.

Your Commercial Will Set You Apart

There's more to a winning commercial than job titles and positive adjectives. A powerful commercial includes information about how others *benefit* from your services.

What matters is not that you're "the CEO of the XYZ Software Co.," for example, but that you manage a firm whose software helps companies streamline their database operations.

More important than the fact that you're a "financial advisor" is that you help clients increase their income and save time with their investments. Most significant about your position as a paralegal is that you do research for a law firm that helps clients make their cases against the government.

Communicate an effective personal message—one that clearly defines what makes you special and what "only" you offer—and you really will stand out. You will join an elite club—those who can discuss themselves as skillfully as they discuss their products.

These days, it's not enough to be able to talk about your products and services. Let's face it: Customers can get what you offer elsewhere, when they want it, maybe even at the price they want to pay for it.

But there's one thing they can't get elsewhere. They can't get you. Use your personal commercial to point that out.

Action Ideas and Tips

1 **Make your commercial brief.** Say the most you can about yourself in the fewest number of words.

Use action verbs that will help you make a maximum impact with a minimum amount of verbiage.

2 **Make your commercial memorable.** What one thing do you want people to remember about you?

Make that your key criterion for your commercial. Decide on the one fact that you want to be remembered and the one lasting impression you would like to leave.

3 **"So what?"** That's the one question your commercial will have to answer.

Will others *care* about your message? What lasting impact will it have on them? Will it motivate them to act?

If you don't have satisfactory answers to those questions, go back to the drawing board.

4 **Build bridges.** Create logical lead-ins to your commercial, smooth transitions that set the stage for your message without upstaging anyone else. Use lead-ins like "Sounds like I might be able to help you—," or "You and I face similar challenges—," or "The reason I asked that was—."

Those work better than "Let me introduce myself—."

5 **Beat the clock.** Time is short to get your message across. Make the most of it by following these five steps created by Grand Rapids, Michigan consultant Nancy Skinner:
(1) Prepare.
(2) Think before you speak.
(3) Get straight to the point in your first sentence.
(4) Give your listener guidelines ("I'd like to cover three points") and stick to them.
(5) Less is better. Keep your message simple.
(6) Recap your main points.

6 **Tell what "only" you can do.** Highlight your uniqueness by including an "only" in your commercial, as in "I am the only...."

Back it up by drawing from your expertise, personal history, and any career highlight that sets you apart. Use words like "special" and "unique" to get your point across.

7 **Define your differences.** Determine how you stand out by completing the following:
- What makes me different from others in my profession is...
- What makes me different from others in my field is...

- What makes me different from others in my industry is...
- What makes me different from others in my company is...
- What makes me different from others in my sales territory is...
- What makes me different from others in my community is...
- What makes me different from others in my age group is...
- What makes me different from others with my experience is...
- What makes me different from others serving my market is...

8 **Put some muscle into your USP.** A powerful Unique Selling Proposition singles out your products and services.
Create one covering:
- how your business is operated
- how your product is developed
- how it's manufactured or marketed
- how it's delivered, etc.

—Jeff Blackman in *Entrepreneur* magazine

9 **Show why you're the one, the only...you!** Determine your uniqueness by identifying ways you're....
- Unconventional
- Singular
- Rare
- Novel
- Incomparable
- Exceptional

10 **Speak of your specialty.** Differentiate yourself by identi-

fying how and where you specialize. Describe your special services, your special clients, etc.

11 **Promote results.** In your commercial, refer to a few past accomplishments. Cite your track record as proof that you've done what you say you can do. Share examples of how you've increased revenues, cut costs, and so forth.

12 **Adapt your benefits.** Point out your most unique benefits, then arrange them in your message in order of importance to the buyer.
—*Getting Business to Come to You* by Paul & Sarah Edwards and Laura Clampitt Douglas

13 **Show how you do good, and do away with the bad.** Add clout to your commercial by showing how you can increase desired conditions, and reduce undesirable ones.

Telephone sales expert Art Sobczak lists some of each:

Desired words: profits, sales, revenue, income, cash flow, savings, productivity, morale, motivation, output, attitude, victories, market share

Undesired words: costs, trouble, problems, restrictions, obstacle, expenses, charge, taxes, hassle, burden, drudgery, inconvenience, annoyance

14 **Limit your points—more than three's a crowd.** Including four or more benefits makes your commercial confusing. So contends Morey

Stettner in his book *The Art of Winning Conversation*. Stettner adds that most people can't digest more than three concise points.

He says that's why so many advertising slogans follow the three-beat: "The few, the proud, the Marines;" "Reduce, reuse, recycle;" "Smiles, service and samples" (See's Candies); and "Fast, friendly, free delivery" (Domino's Pizza).

15 **Avoid weak openers.** Self-defeating words can weaken your case before you have the chance to make it.

Also, avoid opening lines that focus on your reasons for meeting with prospects, rather than on the benefits to them.

Here's what NOT to say when contacting a prospect, according to Lee Boyan in *Successful Cold Call Selling*:

"Sorry to bother you, but..."

"Is this a bad time?"

"I'd like to get an appointment with you..."

"I just happened to be in the neighborhood..."

"I was wondering if you might be interested in..."

"I wanted to visit with you for a few minutes about..."

"I'd like to get your business..."

16 **Apologies not accepted.** Don't seek forgiveness for your "shortcomings." Reframe your message in positive terms:

Instead of saying...	Say...
"Excuse my messy office..."	"Welcome."
"Let's take my car, if you don't mind riding in a clunker."	"Let's take my car."
"It's only my opinion, and I could be wrong..."	" I believe..."
"I'm just the receptionist and I probably won't be able to help you..."	"I'm the receptionist and I'll be happy to help you..."
"I just got lucky..."	"I worked hard and my efforts paid off..."
"I failed..."	"Here's what I learned..."

—Power Talking: 50 Ways to Say What You Mean and Get What You Want by George Walther

17 **"Develop" alternatives.** So many people use the word "develop" to describe their accomplishments. Here are substitutes for your commercial:

Create	Construct	Introduce
Design	Coordinate	Organize
Establish	Cultivate	Originate
Implement	Devise	Perfect
Institute	Enhance	Pioneer
Introduce	Fashion	Plan
Set up	Form	Produce
Built	Generate	Prepared
Compose	Install	Refine

—Resume Power: Selling Yourself on Paper by Tom Washington

18 **Enliven your message with action words.** Consider these:

Train	Manage
Improve	Present
Analyze	Organize
Direct	Administer
Supervise	Conduct
Invent	Complete
Expand	Launch
Plan	Eliminate
Arrange	Change
Unleash	Prepare
Update	Increase
Clarify	Compile

—*Over 40 and Looking for Work?*
by Rebecca Jespersen Anthony
and Gerald Roe

19 **Add commitments to your commercial.** Use your message to show what you're dedicated to. Whether it's superior customer service, cutting-edge technology, or computer literacy—your commercial is a good way to announce it.

20 **Accept credit for your awards.** Use "award-winning" in your commercial if ever you've received an award. You're an "award-winning marketing director," for example, if you were honored for a brochure design.

21 **Show how you help.** How and who you help means more than your job title or description.
Use your commercial to identify the ways you assist others (e.g., "I help homeowners save money by...").

22 **Create a slogan.** Identify yourself as a "fruit wholesaler," and you may not catch anyone's attention. Call yourself "The Mango Man," and you will.
A good nickname will get you noticed and remembered.

23 **Break the ice with the gatekeeper.** Modify your message to make a positive impression on receptionists, secretaries, and other screeners.
Devise a commercial for them with reasons why they should connect you with the boss. (*"I have some examples of how Ms. Jones can increase the amount of corporate sponsorship your company receives."*)

24 **Try before you buy.** Test out your commercial on mentors, advisors, clients, family and friends. Fine tune your message based on their feedback.

25 **Take a time-out.** Interrupt a product presentation for your personal commercial.
It will convince your prospect that she won't just get your product when she buys from you, she'll get YOU!

26 **Finish strong.** The close of your commercial is the part others will remember. Conclude with words that will maintain their interest (for example, "I've helped the Sanders, OXY, and Pilbro corporations double their market share. I can do the same for you.").

27 **Make midcourse corrections.** Revisit, review, and update your personal commercial every few months. As your market, clients, products and services change, so should your message.

28 **Relish, then relinquish the spotlight.** Present your commercial with full gusto, but then focus your attention on your "audience."

Dwelling on your commercial can dilute its impact. When you communicate an effective personal message, the focus is sure to return to it—and you.

29 **Get "talkers" talking about you.** If you can't get back the spotlight after giving it up, try a graceful interruption.

Try agreeing with the speaker and linking his comments to your commercial. Or cut in with a question that redirects the conversation to your commercial.

—L.C. Williams & Associates, Chicago-based public relations firm, quoted in *Investors Business Daily*

30 **Get the team to talk the talk.** Make sure everyone in the office communicates your commercial correctly. Post it, script it or do what ever else is necessary to teach the staff to say the right stuff.

31 **Talk your talk, not your predecessor's.** A customer may want to discuss previous performance when you take over the account from a predecessor or competitor. But switch the focus to the benefits and services *you'll* provide.

—*The Working Communicator* newsletter

32 **Ask questions.** Good questions let you control the flow of the conversation. At the same time, you learn about the prospect's needs AND they think you're a great conversationalist!

33 **Keep it fresh.** However many times you recite your commercial, most individuals hear it only once. Sound enthusiastic and your message will sound new and spontaneous. Canned commercials get ignored.

34 **Customize your commercial.** Adapt your message to fit different circumstances and different audiences. The version you use at a professional conference should differ from the networking event version.

35 **Massage your message.** Replace the "closed" sign with the one that reads "We reopen at 9 a.m." Don't tell buyers not to return items after 30 days. Tell them you'll gladly accept refunds within 30 days of purchase. Don't mention the 10 percent of the models you don't service. Focus on the 90 percent that you do.

36 **When in doubt, leave it out.** Ponder public perceptions. If your profession, title, or company name triggers negative stereotypes, avoid using them. If the term "salesman" turns off those you seek to influence, use "account manager" instead.

37 **Tabulate your talking points.** Create discussion topics to supplement your message. Include fast facts and points of interest about yourself along with examples of your recent achievements.

38 **Deliver the goods now.** Make your products or services available to a new customer immediately. That gets your relationship off to a good start, and lessens the chances the customer will change his mind and call off the deal.

39 **Recruit an "introducer."** Somebody knows everybody at virtually every networking event.
   Introduce yourself to that somebody, and ask her to introduce you to others. That way, you can share your commercial with the right people in a short amount of time.

40 **Introduce ideas on how to introduce you.** Provide "introducers" with a simple script that accentuates the positive about you. Prepare them, whether they're going to introduce your speech or introduce you to others at a networking event.

41 **Make your e-mail address memorable.** A little imagination goes a long way. Do something creative!

42 **Use your voice mail to market yourself.** Add a promotional note to your telephone message ("Hi, you've reached Joan Doakes, a recent winner of the company's 'Agent of the Month' award").
   Use a different promotional note in each of the "mailboxes" in your phone system.

43 **Use your voice mail to market your expertise.** Include a voice mail information line option advising callers on industry trends, new technology, etc. A mortgage lender, for example, could offer advice on timing your loan application.
   It will motivate some prospects to call you, and others to call you more often.

44 **Offer a longer voice-mail version.** Telemarketing expert Margie Seyfer recommends the following five-step voice mail cycle:
(1) Begin with a greeting that thanks the caller for contacting you, and identifies you and your company. ("Thanks for calling Power Promotion. This is Fred Berns.") Offer the caller the option to skip ahead or leave a message immediately.
(2) Describe the products and services that your company offers. ("We offer programs and products designed to help companies increase their profits by marketing themselves more effectively.")
(3) Ask one or two pain questions. ("Are you falling short of your financial goals? Do you have a difficult time differentiating your company from competitors?")
(4) State the advantages of doing business with your company. ("Our customized presentations and per-

sonal promotion consultation can help you communicate with confidence, set yourself apart from competitors and develop a marketing action plan.")

(5) Close by repeating your gratitude for the call. ("We look forward to returning your call. Thanks again for calling Power Promotion.")

45 **Include voice-mail outcomes before options.** List results first. "To learn more about our 'try before you buy' plan, press two" is easier to remember than "Press two for the 'try before you buy' plan."

46 **Get 'em sold as they hold.** If you have to put callers on hold, expose them to prerecorded promotional information. It's an old trick, but it works.

Inbound/Outbound magazine estimates that 85 percent of callers on hold will stay on the line if a message is offered. That's significant, considering that 70 percent of all callers to businesses are placed on hold.

47 **Follow your commercial with a card.** Share your commercial at a networking event, and you get your message across. Distribute your business card with it, and you reinforce it—and pave the way for a future contact.

48 **Follow your meeting with a memo.** Your commercial may be great, but the memory of those you share it with may not be as good. Fol-

low a face-to-face meeting with a note that repeats your personal commercial.

49 **If it bears your name, it should bear your commercial.** Include some form of your commercial every time you create a marketing piece. That goes for everything from business cards to postcards, from one-sheets to fax cover sheets, from newsletters to news releases.

50 **Put your message on your "mug."** Attach your personal message to each of your promotional photos. That beats just including your name with a photo. Send the printed commercial along with the photo to a publication, and the editors may use it as a photo caption.

CHAPTER TWO

Document Your Deeds

"Men are like in their promises.
It is only in their deeds that they differ."
—Molière

I f only you could sell yourself with words alone. If only you could sit back and rely on a few well-chosen words to make your dreams come true—words that would close deals, dramatically increase your income, influence decision makers, win you fame and acclaim, and assure that you'll live happily ever after.

But talk is cheap. Words alone won't get you where you want to go. You can't just *say* you're good. You need to back up your words with deeds.

Tally Your Successes

That should be easy to do. Every day you're responsible for important actions. You sell and create products and services that improve the quality of people's lives. You help increase your company's profits. You accomplish tasks, solve problems, overcome obstacles, achieve goals, and reach milestones.

You do so much. But chances are that you under-value and even disregard your deeds.

People tend to forget their own accomplishments. Most are hard pressed to recall a few of their achievements of the past

> "Man, unlike any other thing organic or inorganic in the universe, grows be-yond his work, walks up the stairs of his concepts, emerges ahead of his accomplishments."
> —John Steinbeck

week or month. Many struggle to pinpoint the key achievements in their careers.

It's a different story when you ask people about their failures and disappointments. Many can cite examples of what *hasn't* worked, or the goals they didn't reach.

Overlooking personal achievement is a widespread problem. But a problem is nothing more than the difference between what you have and what you need. And what you need here is to keep track of your successes.

Simple, isn't it? All you have to do is write down what works, record your victories, and spread the word about them. One way to do this is to share news about the goals you reach and the missions you accomplish. Focus on results—the positive outcomes of your efforts. Zero in on the sales increases, rates of growth, expanded market share, productivity improvements, reduced expenditures, and other changes that you help bring about.

The more you communicate with your clients, the easier it will be for you to monitor your progress. By inquiring about the outcomes of your efforts, you'll show that you really care about the success of those you serve.

Make Self-Promotion a Habit

Chances are, you're not in the habit of chronicling your achievements. Most likely you have a resume, perhaps a brochure, maybe even a Web page. But selling yourself in general—and documenting your success in particular—probably isn't something that comes "naturally" to you.

Personal promotion is not a skill with which we're born. Self-promotion is one of life's great equalizers:

Everyone needs to do it, yet no one comes into the world with an innate sense of *how* to do it.

Self-promotion is a learned behavior—a critically important learned behavior. Devote a few minutes each day to documenting your deeds and logging your accomplishments, and you will shorten your learning curve.

How you do it doesn't matter. Jot down ideas in a loose-leaf binder. Create a computer file. Keep a notebook. Scribble notes to yourself, and stick them in a shoe box. Do whatever it takes to maintain a written record of your accomplishments and achievements.

The routine here is nearly as important as the result. You'll create a habit. Take notes daily, and you'll get in the habit of becoming your own personal historian. You'll become accustomed to observing your own performance, to watching out for your every productive action. It will become second nature to you to keep tabs on your contributions.

And a worthwhile habit it is! You'll create a record that will enable you and others to recognize and appreciate your accomplishments.

Build Your Resume

Your record should include information about what you *can* do, as well as what you have done.

Provide a guide to your capabilities and skills, updating it regularly as you acquire more technical, administrative, managerial, and other know-how. Keep track of your educational experiences: seminars, workshops, outside training, coaching sessions and other skill-enhancing educational activities.

Create a worthy record, and others will say that it "speaks for itself." That's welcome news if you're the kind of individual who is more comfortable expressing your accomplishments on paper than in person.

Recording your accomplishments will set you apart from your competitors in more ways than one. For one thing, you'll do something that most of those competitors don't do.

In addition, the personal record keeping will convince *you* that you are an original. Review your records, and you'll realize that your attributes, capabilities, and skills are uniquely yours. No one has achieved exactly what you have, in the way you have. No one has the same personal history, educational background, and experience as you.

That realization will increase your appreciation of yourself. It will enhance your ability to make the personal sale, even under the most challenging circumstances.

Chart Your Performance

Account for your accomplishments, large and small. Include the sales you close, the cost-cutting steps you take, the changes you initiate, the deals you arrange, the innovations you introduce, the goals you reach, the recognition you receive, and the honors and awards you win.

Put your performance into perspective. Chart your rate of growth. Compare your performance to your own in past years, and to that of your competitors today.

Document your organization's progress as well as your own. A member of a profitable company, or any other winning team, commands respect. The better you can make your company look, the better *you* will look.

Documentation Pays

Documenting your deeds will take time. So what's the payoff for all this paperwork?

The payoff will be a record—a track record in print. It will be a record that can work wonders for you if you continually update it, review it prior to key meetings or presentations, and treat it as the vital resource that it is.

It *will* work wonders if you adapt it to fit different circumstances. Share from your record only that information which is most relevant to each audience. To communicate most effectively, avoid unnecessary detail.

Your record speaks for you in good times and bad. It sells you, even on those occasions when you don't feel up to selling yourself. It's your personal "textbook," your weapon and the verification of your value.

The record lends truth to your personal advertising and credence to your self-promotion efforts. It spells out the benefits others receive when they invest in you. It explains to customers what they got for their money.

In this high-tech, highly competitive era, customers want "the facts, nothing but the facts." They want you to "show 'em the money." They want you to put up, or shut up. They want proof that you have done for others what you say you can do for them.

Those are all good reasons why you should document your deeds. Here's another one: Customers aren't as easily impressed as they once were.

Customers Have Many Options

Your customers and prospects can choose from more alternatives than ever before. If they're dissatisfied with your service, they can seek out your local competitors. If that doesn't work, they can go online and track down still more resources, including mail order vendors.

Today's customers are like kids in candy stores, exposed to a multitude of options and not particularly loyal to any one of them. Consequently, they have short memories and are more insistent than ever about knowing "whaddya done for me lately?"

You must be concise and consistent in your answer to that question. You must let them know precisely how you can help them.

You can communicate that information in any number of ways: from a personal note to a newsletter, from

a weekly phone call to an annual report. Think of your customers as shareholders in your
personal corporation to whom
you must be fully accountable.

Accounting for your actions
makes for good customer relations and good business. Document and share your deeds, and
you will validate your fee, and
demonstrate why you're worth the price.

Your record is the paper trail that you can use to
substantiate your success and bolster your image in
the public eye. Your record will have the most impact if
you include with it the names of persons who can vouch
for you. Put together a reference list of customers, industry leaders, and anyone else who can speak in your
behalf.

Self-Presentations Prepare You

When you want to raise your fee, or receive a higher
salary, your record makes it easier to do.

Here's a homework assignment for you: Create a
presentation in which you ask for more money. Design
it as a speech to your clients justifying your rate hike.

What makes this exercise so valuable is that it forces
you to take stock—to review your Winner's Workbook
and extract the most relevant successes.

You may not need that presentation now, but you
will some day. Collect your facts now—before you need
them.

Commit to memory your most significant recent
achievements. Incorporate them into a presentation, using a script at first, and rehearsing in front of a mirror
or video camera.

Transform your achievements into talking points
to which you can easily refer in networking, prospecting, or sales situations. Spice up your presentation with
tales from the trenches, stories about offbeat, humor-

ous, and memorable experiences you encountered along the way to accomplishing your mission.

Spin Control

Facts can make you or break you in a performance review. Someday, somewhere, you'll find yourself across  the table from your boss, or a major client, at a review session.

Your mission: to put the best possible spin on your performance. Your chances for success: good if you've maintained a list of your achievements, poor if you haven't.

The more you practice making the personal sale, the more adept you will become at spin control. That's the fine art of finding the good and accentuating the positive, even in seemingly negative circumstances.

Spin control is discussing the positive rate of growth, even when sales are lackluster. It's focusing on the deal you recently signed, rather than on the contracts that fell through. It's emphasizing the money you saved at a time when earnings were down.

Spin control requires careful scrutiny and, in some cases, an active imagination. Examine your personal record from enough angles, and you're sure to find positive statistics to report.

Your record also provides you with ammunition to use against external skeptics and internal doubts. You may need all the documentation you can get to overcome the critic within you.

All too often self-doubt limits the degree to which some professionals promote themselves. The doubt may be linked to a past setback: the loss of a sale, the collapse of a contract, the bankruptcy of a business, the failure to gain a promotion, the wasting of an opportunity. Years may have passed since that setback, but they continue to stew about what could have been.

Self-doubt robs people of their self-confidence and sours their spirits. These doubters are the ones who most need, but are least likely, to document and appreciate their achievements.

> "If you want to be successful, know what you are doing, love what you are doing, and believe in what you are doing."
>
> —Will Rogers

Fail Your Way to Success

Don't give "failure" a bad rap. Don't let fear of failure prevent you from learning from it.

Rather than dwell on setbacks, keep a list of lessons you learn from them. That list belongs in your Winner's Workbook and in your computer.

When the going gets toughest, refer to your record of achievements. It will lift your spirits and restore your confidence. One glance at your performance chart can give meaning and purpose to your daily routine.

Your performance record reveals results. Those results provide answers to questions you and others may have about why you do what you do.

Numerous failures preceded the success of some of our most famous heroes. Thomas Edison invented the light bulb after failing to do so 10,000 times. Clearly, he applied what he learned from his setbacks.

Many of life's most successful individuals are those who have failed the most. Past setbacks are the building blocks of future triumphs.

"Failure does not exist," writes Wayne Dyer in his book, *Your Erroneous Zones.* "Failure is simply someone else's opinion of how a certain act should have been completed."

Some of the most prosperous sales representatives are the ones who are most accustomed to hearing "no." Sid Friedman, the president of a Philadelphia insurance, financial planning, and consulting firm, was in the top tenth of one percent of all insurance salespeople in the world in the mid-1990s. He earned commissions of more than $2.6 million a year—despite the fact that 85 of 100 people he contacted each week turned him down.

Getting Past "No"

How many "nos" can you take? How many times have you wanted to go up and talk to someone you found attractive, then decided not to do it because you didn't want to hear the word "no"? How many of you decided not to try for a job or make a sales call or audition for a part because you didn't want to be rejected? Think about how crazy that is. Think how you're creating limits just because of your fear of that little two-letter word. The word itself has no power. It can't cut your skin or sap your strength. Its power comes from the way you represent it to yourself. It's power comes from the limits it make you create. And what do limited thoughts create? Limited lives.

So when you learn to run your brain, you can learn to handle rejection. You can even anchor yourself so the word "no" turns you on. You can take any rejection and turn it into an opportunity. If you're in telephone sales, you can anchor yourself so that simply reaching for the phone puts you in ecstasy rather than raising the fear of rejection. Remember, success is buried on the other side of rejection.

There are no real successes without rejection. The more rejection you get, the better you are, the more you've learned, the closer you are to your outcome. The next time somebody rejects you, you might give him a hug. That'll change his physiology. Turn "nos" into hugs. If you can handle rejection, you'll learn to get everything you want.

—Tony Robbins

But he understood that if he could get those 15 appointments, he could sell three. "Sell three per week," he said. "Earn lots of money. It's that simple."

Positive, Future Focus

Successful self-promoters focus on the "From now on..." time frame. They channel their energy into future goals and marketing strategies. They need only to review their written records to remind themselves that they have succeeded before and can—and will—do so again.

Fear of failure is a formidable stumbling block for some

"The best way to predict the future is to create it."
—Peter Drucker

professionals. The fear is characterized by uncertainty—uncertainty over future financial stability, over whether their new products will catch on, over their jobs following a merger.

Sadly, one of the first things to go when their self-confidence ebbs is their personal marketing efforts. Once they stop feeling good about themselves, they stop promoting themselves.

Here's when they most need to fall back on a written record of their successes

Write, Write, Write

Never stop writing *your* personal record. It will enable you to promote yourself in the darkest hours. It will pave the way for tomorrow's success. It will prepare you for, and protect you from, change.

Things change; that's a certainty. Technology changes. Your market and customer base change. Your career changes an average of four to six times, studies show. One thing that remains constant is your record of achievement. No one can take away from you what you've accomplished, providing you've maintained a record of your accomplishments.

A commitment to document your deeds and acknowledge your successes lessens the likelihood that you'll give in to two destructive and debilitating emotions: regret and fear. Those two emotions force executives and employees alike to focus on negative outcomes that are done and gone, or those that have yet to take place.

> "Regret and fear are twin thieves that would rob of us today."
> —Robert J. Hastings

Dwelling on negative thoughts of yesterday and tomorrow reduces your effectiveness today. It reduces your self-confidence and weakens your resolve to promote yourself.

Keep a Journal

A Winner's Workbook can restore your resolve.

That kind of personal journal—call it a "logbook" or "diary," if you'd like—can be the ultimate "yes, you can!" resource. It's the kind of brain food that instills uplifting thoughts and a favorable self-image.

Positive thinking is SO important to selling yourself. A positive mental outlook is the cornerstone of successful self-promotion.

For years personal growth specialists have linked what you conceive and believe to what you can achieve. As motivation expert Earl Nightengale put it: "You are what you think about."

You and you alone decide whether to let positive thoughts guide your actions. The only way that negative developments and words can affect you is if you let them. Only you can get you down.

Document and promote the value of who you are and what you do, and you'll capture the attention of those you seek to influence. Promote your accomplishments and your capabilities, and you'll substantially increase the demand for your services. Promote what makes you different, and you'll establish yourself in a class *by* yourself.

Think Positively and Success Will Follow

An accountant I knew questioned whether his practice was worth promoting. "Look, I'm a lone eagle, a one-man band," he said. "I'm not exactly one of the Big Six accounting firms...not like Arthur Andersen. That's the problem."

That's not the problem," I replied. "That's the *point.* You're somebody who's different from anybody else. That means your firm is different, too. That's worth promoting."

Self-doubt and self-promotion don't mix. You must overcome doubt, accentuate your positives, and become an inner winner *before* you can develop your personal promotion plan. If you don't believe that your services are worth promoting, neither will your clients and prospects.

Documenting *your* deeds—regularly recording your achievements and charting your progress—will convince you that you are worth promoting. It forces you to give yourself credit where credit is due and to realize that you *already are* successful.

Define Your Goals for Success

Too many people look on success as a final destination, and they view their careers as a desperate quest to reach it. That most people aren't as successful as they'd like to be has less to do with their abilities than the fact that they fail to identify the destination. They fail to determine what it is they consider to be success.

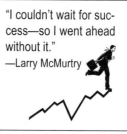

"I couldn't wait for success—so I went ahead without it."
—Larry McMurtry

That's why it's so important to determine what success means to you, to base your mission on it, and to include your mission statement in your Winner's Workbook.

Success is a subjective judgment, not a definite set of circumstances or station to be reached at some point in your journey.

"How restlessly we pace the aisles, damning the minutes for loitering...waiting, waiting, waiting for the station," writes Robert J. Hastings in *The Station.* "However, sooner or later, we must realize there is no one station, no one place to arrive at once and for all. The true joy in life is in the trip."

Others can't determine whether or when you are successful. That's your job. You are the one who decides on your personal goals, and you are the one who knows when you accomplish them.

Surely, you already have accomplished some of the goals

If You Work at Home

Personal record keeping is especially important to the growing number of professionals who work at home. For them, there's no traditional office where they can showcase their talents and receive recognition.

More than 60 million people were involved in some kind of home-based work as of the year 2000. Not only are more of us working for ourselves, more of us are working *by* ourselves.

If you are, or will be one of them, get going on your Winner's Workbook immediately. It's a powerful validation tool, whether you run a business from your home, telecommute or simply finish the work you bring home from your office.

you set for yourself earlier in your career. Therefore, you already are successful.

As for those goals you haven't yet achieved —that certain level of income or new job or degree —you're in the process of achieving them. You have succeeded in making a commitment to successfully reach your goals.

Diligently record your daily accomplishments, and you'll be able to chart your progress toward the achievement of your goals.

Document Your Effect on Others

Recording your daily accomplishments creates a paper trail that substantiates your success. The notes you keep in a daily log, a workbook, or a file lend truth to your personal advertising and credence to your self-promotion efforts.

Keeping a written record of your achievements is a service not only to yourself, but to those you serve. Your record chronicles the work you've performed, and identifies the responsibilities and tasks that you can take on. It educates others on the return they receive for investing in you.

Your record tells the "rest" of your story, providing data that can supplement, or perhaps even supersede information that others have about you.

An executive at a cabinet manufacturing firm may only know that his company's gross sales haven't substantially increased since it began buying your company's custom door handles.

But, say you interview the firm's service manager and discover that customer complaints have dropped dramatically since the firm began distributing your handles. You find out that the company's installers have experienced a 75 percent reduction in service calls, and have filed 50 percent fewer overtime claims.

Share the "rest of story" with the executive, and he will appreciate your business far more.

Promote Yourself—No One Else Will

Failure to keep and share your personal record can be costly—as D.T. Harvey discovered.

Harvey, the vice president of a major New York food concern, helped turn around a troubled division within the organization. He restructured the work force to boost productivity, introduced sales incentives to bolster sagging revenue, and created a new product line.

"I sweated blood over this division," Harvey said. "I thought everyone would see my diligence."

He chose not to describe his work, but instead talked to his bosses about topics like improving market conditions and a more productive work force.

The result? The company fired him from his $150,000-a-year post.

"They thought the division improved on its own," Harvey observed. "They thought it was the economy. They didn't realize how hard I worked over that unit, and that if it hadn't been for some drastic measures taken on my part, we could have lost it. In retrospect, I guess they had no way of really knowing what all I did. I never let them know."

Harvey violated a cardinal rule of self-promotion: You can prosper if you become known. You won't if you don't.

The moral of his story: Don't make assumptions. Never assume those you seek to influence, or anyone else for that matter, know what you do, what you have done and what you can do.

Never assume that you don't have to promote yourself, that others will understand and appreciate your efforts. Keep your accomplishments to yourself, and you'll pay the consequences.

"When working for a company, don't assume that people will automatically notice your accomplishments," warns Celia D. Crossley, a career strategist and human resources consultant in Columbus, Ohio. "Talk about your accomplishments in a proud way. Try to use the same tone you would use in announcing a wedding or a birth."

Documenting your accomplishments simplifies the task of self-promotion. It's one thing to call yourself a unique, one-of-a-kind professional. It's another thing to prove it.

Personal Selling Always Pays Off

Keeping track of your achievements certainly will add power to your personal selling efforts. It's not, however, a guarantee that you'll always be successful in those efforts.

Successful or not, your personal selling efforts will always pay off. That's because whenever you promote yourself, you win even when you "lose." Each time you accentuate your positives and blow your own horn, you hone your self-marketing presentation.

Each time you promote yourself, you create an impression and you increase the chance that you will be remembered the next time.

You'll learn in Chapter 6 about how to pitch a story about yourself or your business to the news media. Again your success is not guaranteed; the reporter you contact may choose not to run your story. Even so, he or she is more likely to remember you the *next* time you call.

I wish I could promise you that you will close every personal sale you attempt. I can't. Your success in personal sales is no sure thing.

But you can enhance your odds for success by implementing the strategies in this book. Among the most important of those strategies is documenting your deeds.

Maintain records of your achievements, and you'll be able to verify your value and substantiate your success. That, alone, should vault you ahead of your competitors.

Action Ideas and Tips

51 **Develop a Winner's Workbook.** Your workbook is your success diary—a repository for your daily achievements. Include information on your:

- accomplishments
- contributions to your company
- missions and projects successfully completed
- goals attained
- skills learned
- problems solved
- innovative solutions to challenges
- sales achievements

52 **Map out your mission.** Set forth your long-term goal in your Winner's Workbook.

Defining your "destination" will help you identify your successes. Activities which move you closer to that destination are worth noting.

Refer often to your mission, and you'll find more direction and purpose in your daily activities.

53 **Chart monthly goals.** Create monthly objectives, and record your success in achieving them. This demonstrates your diligence and your commitment to excellence.

54 **Take time to take stock.** Schedule time each week to document your deeds. Consider blocking out an hour on Friday to review and record key accomplishments during the previous seven days. The schedule will help you appreciate your performance, and will give you a positive boost for the weekend.

55 **Monitor your milestones.** As a self-promoter, you are your own personal historian. It's your duty, therefore, to keep track of the numbers: the years you've been on the job, customers you've served, the sales you've closed, etc.

Milestones make you memorable. Keep track of yours.

56 **Use your daytimer for documentation.** Jot down success stories in your daily calendar book so you don't forget about them later. Instant record keeping assures that you won't lose track of your achievements.

Refresh your memory by adding notations in your calendar book next to appointment listings—indicating the *outcomes* of those appointments.

57 **Use your Web page to share your successes.** Add news of your latest accomplishments to your Web page, and update the information regularly. Include brief accounts of how clients and others have benefited from your products and services. Testimonial comments from satisfied customers increase your credibility even more.

58 **Put deeds in the database.** Keep track of who you've helped, and how, by recording benefit information after the names on your database.

Include notes on at least one benefit that each individual has received as a result of your association.

59 **Adapt your deeds to their needs.** Be selective in the accomplishments you share with the individuals you seek to impress. You risk losing their attention if you recount achievements that they find irrelevant.

Know enough about those individuals to know which of your deeds would mean most to them.

60 **Use success stories to reinforce new relationships.** As you welcome new customers, share with them some of your recent success stories.

This will assure them of your value and track record, and assure them that they made the right decision in choosing to work with you.

61 **Find out how others find out about you.** "How did you hear about us?" You've been asked that question countless times, but do *you* ask that question? Only by listening to the answers can you do the best job of evaluating your personal marketing. You don't have unlimited time to spend on self-promotion, so you need to determine the best use of your time.

62 **Make sure others hear the cheers.** Let others know every time your efforts are acknowledged. Get the word out about honors, awards, positive customer feedback, praise from your boss, publicity in an in-house publication, or any other form of recognition you receive.

Recognition gives you credibility and helps you make your case at annual reviews, board meetings and other forums where attention is focused on your performance.

63 **Make a big deal of the little things.** Don't keep a secret of the favors, freebies, and extras that you make available to those you serve.

Promote your add-ons and value-added services. When you donate your services, enclose "courtesy discount" invoices showing what the normal fees would be, and accounting for the hours you invested at no cost. The result: The recipients will more greatly value your service.

—Keeping Clients Satisfied by Robert W. Bly

64 **Preserve past projects.** Hold on to the best of your reports, proposals, work samples, blueprints, executive summaries, and other documents.

Those materials substantiate your success, demonstrate your expertise, and educate your prospects about what you can do for them.

65 **Preserve client materials.** File one marketing piece from each of your clients.

This archive will help you respond to questions about your past experience. It's one thing to simply throw out a name, but quite another to share written information about a firm you've served.

Brochures, newsletters, annual reports or other materials from your clients are worth saving.

66 **Let others help create your story.** Don't rely on *your* memory alone to reconstruct your success record.

Ask family, friends, associates, and good customers for memories, impressions, and ideas that you can add to your Winner's Workbook. They may be recall accomplishments that you overlooked.

67 **Play photographer.** Pictures help you create a photographic record within your Winner's Workbook.

Photograph the people and places you encounter along your road to fame and fortune. Photos help verify your success and remind you of goals achieved and lessons learned. In addition to verifying your record, the pictures can trigger positive recollections and emotions.

68 **Work with wish lists.** Ask your customers and others you work with to share their goals, and then document your efforts to help achieve them. Notify them each time you fulfill one of their objectives, and provide them with regular progress reports on the others.

69 **Outline the outcomes.** Track down the outcomes of your efforts by asking clients to share positive results of your services. Focus on sales and productivity increases and other outcomes attributable to your products or services.

Those results bolster your track record and offer proof of the return on the investment that you offer.

70 **Account for accomplishments before increasing prices.** Never propose a price hike before discussing your achievements.

Run down a list of benefits your customers have received from your services before announcing the additional cost for them in the future.

71 **Look back.** Stay connected with those to whom you're accountable by providing periodic summaries of your services. Review your activities over the past month or quarter or year. List them in order of importance, in chronological order, or in some other logical sequence. Create a written report which you can present in person.

Careful documentation of deeds along the way simplifies the task of pulling together the information for your presentation.

72 **Look ahead.** Share your vision for the future.

Preview your goals for your relationship with a customer, a prospect, or anyone else you seek to influence. Focus on future projects and the results you expect. Supply information about new skills, technology, and expertise you've acquired, and how you'll use them in the future.

73 **Stage a mutual-appreciation event.** Invite your best customers, mentors, and others to an event at which you thank them for their help. Use the occasion to make sure they appreciate you, as well. Share news of your success, reminding them of the ways in which they benefit from your services.

74 **Outline the obstacles.** Your record of achievement is all the more meaningful if you include the challenges you overcame along the way.

Account for the problems, setbacks, negative circumstances, crises, and other adverse conditions on your road to success. Describe the strategies you used to turn your career lemons into lemonade.

75 **Tell it like it was.** To put your accomplishments in perspective, describe conditions before you arrived. Share information about your clients' needs and problems, economic conditions, and other factors in place when you came aboard.

76 **Record the reasons why.** Analyze the "whys" and "wherefores" of your achievements.

Probing your success is as valuable as analyzing your setbacks. For one thing, it will remove some of the uncertainty around future goal achievement.

77 **Keep an eye on your spin-offs.** Keep track of where your sales come from. Often they're a by-product of service you performed earlier for someone else.

Documenting these spin-offs will help you understand what's working for you.

78 **Document your differences.** Tracking your accomplishments should help you differentiate yourself from your competitors. After all, no one has achieved precisely what you have.

Record these differences at your every opportunity. These insights will serve as useful sales tools as you promote yourself in the future.

79 **Categorize your conquests.** Create "skill categories" for your accomplishments.

Some examples: management, communications, selling, supervision, coordination, planning, conflict management, motivation, administration, production, problem solving, negotiating, evaluating, etc.

—*Career Power* by Richard Rinella and Claire Robbins

80 **Document your team's triumphs.** Making your company look good makes you look good.

Collect your colleagues' success stories, and share them with those you seek to influence. It will give your company — and you — a winning image.

81 **Document defeats—and lessons learned.** What matters when things don't work out is not what you lose, but what you learn.

Worth noting are insights gained from setbacks. Keep records of the lessons you take away from lost sales, broken contracts, unsuccessful negotiations, firings, and other reversals.

82 **Keep your eyes on the other guys.** Put your own performance in perspective by benchmarking against your competitors. Visit their home page, review their annual reports, consult their vendors—do whatever it takes to measure their progress, or lack thereof.

The more detailed your information, the easier it is to make comparisons.

83 **Create confidence cards.** Prepare for meetings by jotting down on index cards pertinent information about your accomplishments. Adapt the most relevant details to your "audience."

Review your cards en route or in the reception area prior to the meeting.

84 **Report on your progress.** Keep your contacts current by providing them with a quarterly or monthly letter on your latest and greatest achievements. Include any new article reprints, testimonial letters, or related materials.

85 **Keep a "can do" list.** Document your capabilities, qualifications and skills. List the responsibilities that you *can* handle, the duties you're qualified to take on.

Account for your special skills with computers, writing, speaking, administrative, leadership or technical tasks, etc. Draw from your training, educational background and general know-how as well as from your work experience. Share the list with your prospects, clients or boss.

86 **Play the numbers game.** Often, your performance is judged on your numbers: gross sales, net profits, money saved, deals sealed, cases closed, etc.

Include as many relevant statistics as possible in your personal record—and into the information you share with prospects, customers and others.

87 **Chart your progress.** Compare your performance to what it was one, five, or ten years ago. Take into account total sales, net profits, customer numbers, and related statistics.

Many decision makers attach more importance to your rate of growth than any other performance indicator. Monitor that growth rate carefully, and promote it when it serves your purposes.

88 **Chart what's hot.** What are your best-selling products? Which of your services are in greatest demand? Which prospecting technique is bringing in the most business?

Careful record keeping can answer these, and equally important market research questions. Keep statistics in such a way that you can refer to them quickly and often. Use a spreadsheet system or other program that will help you take the guesswork out of your performance.

89 **Chart what's not hot.** Stale inventory, unprofitable services, confusing pricing programs, or outdated return policies can drag you and your company down in a hurry.

Uncover the turkeys in your personal operations and eliminate them immediately. Pay attention to activities which take lots of your time. If they're not making you money, they're costing you money.

90 **Use great verbs to document great deeds.**

Words that cast a favorable light on your accomplishments:

- analyzed
- contracted
- developed
- established
- invented
- negotiated
- presented
- reduced (as in costs)
- researched
- solved
- sold
- supervised
- wrote

(Note: For other "victory verbs," see Chapter 3.)

—*Over 40 and Looking for Work?*
by Rebecca Jespersen Anthony
and Gerald Roe

91 **Keep tabs on "outside" learning experiences.** Keep a record of seminars, workshops, conferences, special projects, and on-the-job training sessions you attend. Add information about after-hours activities: learning to fly a plane, editing a church newsletter, participating in a political campaign, etc.

92 **Tell what else floats your boat.** Keep a record of what you do when the workday is done. List hobbies, recreation, trips, and other extracurricular activities.

Whether you run a local bridge club or you run triathlons, your outside activities are worth noting. Promoting those activities shows that you're a well-rounded individual.

Additionally, your outside activities may open doors for you with prospects and customers who share your interests.

93 **Collect tidbits from the trenches.** Approach life from the light side, and you're sure to accumulate anecdotes, humorous stories, and entertaining tales. Write these down!

Anecdotes can break the ice, put others at ease, and make you more likable. Keep your eyes and ears open for amusing tidbits to add to your anecdote treasure chest.

94 **Put your resume to work for you.** Turn your resume into a marketing tool by using it to elaborate on your achievements rather than simply listing your job experience.

Note that you "achieved 112 percent of your quota as a sales rep for the XYZ Company," rather than merely mentioning that you worked for that company.

Account for accomplishments, describe responsibilities and list the skills you obtained. Include information on significant part-time employment, and on relevant volunteer and community involvement.

—"Resume Writing Requires Proper Strategy" by Sal Divita writing in *Personal Marketing*

95 **Maintain a witness list.** Compile a list of those individuals who witnessed your achievements along the way. Include teachers, supervisors, fellow workers, mentors, customers, and anyone else who can vouch for your past successes. Recontact them, bring them up to date on your current activities, and ask them to serve as references.

Have them jot down their recollections in testimonial letters.

96 **Create calendars.** Inform prospects and others of your schedule for the months ahead. Describe upcoming projects, whom they'll benefit and how. Share your goals and objectives.

A calendar conveys your importance and enhances your image as an expert.

97 **Add triumphant taglines.** Use taglines on your marketing materials and voice mail to document your distinctions. Examples: "Past winner of the 'Cincinnati Minority-Owned Business of the Year' Award;" recipient of "Friends of the Environment Award;" "Official Parts Supplier for the ABC Corporation;" "author of *Trends in High Tech*, etc.

98 **Show who your friends are.** Document your relationships by posting the names of your most prominent customers and contacts in your office—and in your marketing materials.

Get their permission to use their names, then include them in your verbal and print promotion.

99 **Certify your success.** Seek written documentation once you've completed a course, seminar, or work project. Ask for a certificate, letter, transcript, etc.

100 **Write your obituary.** That may sound morbid, but it's an excellent way to keep your career in perspective. It helps you identify your most promotable qualities and memorable achievements, and determine how you want to be remembered.

Revise it along the way so it includes your most recent accomplishments. File it among your personal papers. Consider it a resource that may insure that your message and mission live on.

CHAPTER THREE

Establish Your Expertise

"Everybody is an expert on something."
—Larry King

Want to meet an expert in your field? Look in the mirror.

That's right, the expert is you.

You use many words to introduce and describe yourself but, chances are, "expert" isn't one of them. Why not? It should be.

Consult the dictionary, and you'll see that an expert is defined as "having, involving, or displaying special skill or knowledge derived from training or experience."

You have skill and knowledge. You have experience. You are an expert.

Your challenge is to identify and communicate your expertise in as few words as possible. Complete this sentence: "I'm the expert on..." Or this one: "My area of expertise is..."

There is no better way to express your expertise than to incorporate the word "only" in your personal commercial.

My List of "Onlys"

I'm the only account executive in the firm who...

...has worked for a Fortune 500 company.

Review the "only" principle mentioned in Chapters 1 and 2—then create your own "only" list. It will help you and others appreciate your value as an expert.

Build Your Reputation

Once you define your expertise, you need to demonstrate your track record.

Every expert has a track record, an impressive list of honors and awards recognition received, achievements gained and achieved.

Carefully review your past history, and compile your track record. If you can't recall any awards, you should be able to remember your achievements, your victories, your success stories. Certainly, you can compile a list of the degrees you've earned, and the advanced courses you've completed. Think of these details as building blocks for your reputation.

Craft your reputation carefully, and handle it with care. Beware of missteps along the way that could tarnish that reputation.

Don't just look back as you establish your reputation. Look ahead. Consider your goals for the future. Are you working towards starting a business, earning a degree, achieving a sales milestone (like the Realtors' Million Dollar Roundtable) or writing a book?

By sharing your future objectives with others, you can help fortify your reputation.

Keeping Expert Company

The company you keep is also important to your reputation. Spend enough time with recognized experts, and you will naturally be associated with them. Ultimately, you may be labeled as a friend, associate, or colleague of these experts. Those are good labels to have.

This is not to suggest that you connect with experts in your field primarily because it will enhance your image. Your main reason for hanging out with recognized experts is to learn from them.

You'll create the best learning environment with other experts if you do your homework ahead of time. Check out their Web sites, read their books, review articles written by and about them, interview others about them, and gather any additional information—before you meet with them.

You're not fully prepared for your meeting until you're an expert on the expert.

How better to educate yourself than to study the success secrets of the most successful individuals in your field? Who better to teach you how to rise to the top than the masters?

Think how much expertise you can acquire and how fast you can develop by compiling a list of ideas and success stories of those masters. Talk about shortening your learning curve!

Modeling Others

One of the ways you can mirror the masters is to practice "the power of modeling" that Tony Robbins referred to in his best-selling book, *Unlimited Power.*

"Excellence can be duplicated," Robbins wrote. "If other people can do something, all you need to do is model them with precision and you can do exactly the same thing. If you exactly reproduce someone's actions—both internal and external—then you, too, can produce the same final result."

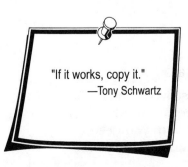

"If it works, copy it."
—Tony Schwartz

It's vital in the modeling process to ask the right questions, and listen—really listen—to the answers. Talk show host Larry King points out that "to be a good talker, you have to be a good listener."

"I realize every morning that nothing I say today will teach me anything," King writes in his book *How to Talk to Anyone, Anytime, Anywhere.* "So if I'm going to learn a lot today, I'll have to do it by listening."

Modeling a master is a shortcut to success. It saves you time and money, and enables you to follow the road and avoid the detours taken by a prominent member of your profession.

Stay Positive

It's important to note that you must play up your own expertise if you are to make the personal sale. That means accentuating all your positives, casting yourself in the best possible light, and communicating your expertise to others. If you don't, no one else will. If you doubt your expertise, so will others.

> "What a man thinks of himself, that is what determines, or rather indicates, his fate."
> —Henry David Thoreau

Be advised that "Dr. No"—your negative inner voice—will balk long and hard at your idea of calling yourself an expert. Let him. Refuse to be swayed by that negativism.

Nor should you be influenced by those who question your expertise, or compare you with those who have gone before you. Try as you will, you may not be able to avoid those who test your knowledge at every opportunity, or compare you to, say, the sales rep who handled your territory before you arrived.

What you can do—what you *must* do—in those circumstances is be your own person and demonstrate your own expertise in your own way. That takes practice.

Project Your Success

First, envision yourself as an "arriver" (someone who already is an expert), rather than a "striver." Then talk the talk, and walk the walk of an expert.

To make your expertise work for you, you need to prove it to others. Your expertise is meaningless if you're the only one who is aware of it. Share information about the awards you've won, the recognition you've received, the milestones you've reached, the articles you've written, and the goals you've achieved.

Let the skeptics say what they want. Their words can't get you down if you don't let them in.

Even so, there will always be those who feel uncomfortable with promoting themselves as "experts." Take the Richmond, Virginia, chiropractor who declared she couldn't consider herself an expert because she's "only been doing this for 11 years now."

She didn't realize that when she had been "doing this" for only 11 days, she had far more expertise than those she served.

Maybe projecting your image as an expert is a stretch you don't feel comfortable making. After a little practice, you will. Whether you're a sales professional or entrepreneur, you can promote yourself as an expert. Accept this idea, believe this idea, embrace this idea, and others will believe it too.

You'll gain public acceptance of your expertise only if you prime the pump. As you share your expertise, promote the fact that you are an expert. That's too important to keep to yourself.

> **The ABCs of Self-Motivation**
>
> **A**djust your attitude
> **B**elieve in yourself.
> **C**hallenge Yourself to do things that you never imagined.
> Have the Commitment to do whatever it takes.
> **D**ream.
>
> —Marilyn Hamilton, founder, Quickie Designs, Inc.

Using Your Value

Your expertise enhances your value considerably. There is greater demand for an expert's service. People attach more value to it—and are willing to pay more for it.

Your expertise distinguishes and differentiates you. It increases your influence and credibility, and enables you to command more respect.

Your expertise positions you as a source and contributes to your image. Once you gain the reputation as an expert, it's difficult to lose it.

But that reputation doesn't come automatically. As always, ya gotta get your name out there.

Publish Your Way to Expert Status

Write articles and you will be perceived as an expert. Pursue the publications that those in your target audience are most likely to read.

Use your articles to address the pain that your customers feel. Also discuss the consequences and offer some (but not all) of the remedies. In so doing, you'll establish or reinforce your image as an expert.

It would be well worth the time of a sales rep for an administrative staffing agency to write an article in a local business journal about the major hiring challenges facing local corporations. She could observe that many companies run inefficiently because they assign full-time account managers to handle clerical duties.

She could point out that several of these companies fall short of their sales goals and fail to turn a profit. And she could cite the long-range consequence of this ineffective staffing approach: Some of these firms go out of business.

The sales rep could conclude the article by recommending a number of staffing solutions—including retaining an administrative staffing agency to handle the more menial tasks.

The rep could give an overview of these and other proposed solutions in her article, and advise readers to obtain additional information by contacting her directly. The article, therefore, could and should attract new business for her, as well as enable her to demonstrate her knowledge.

The saleswoman might be able to accomplish the same goals by writing a letter to the editor of the publication. She would include in the letter the same elements as in the article: problem, ramifications, some remedies.

She could transform the written material into a presentation on the staffing and administrative mistakes of local companies—and how to overcome them. She could then offer the presentation to local business and professional groups who use outside speakers.

Articles and speaking opportunities make excellent vehicles to showcase your expertise. Write and speak often enough, and individuals will pay you to share your time and information with them privately.

The more articles you write, the more material you will accumulate for a book. Those who recognize and admire your expertise want to take a part of you home. That means your advice, articles, books, manuals, pamphlets, tapes, and other materials.

Start packaging your expertise and you can count on some ample "mailbox income" while you sleep.

Be an Information Source

You can create or enhance your image as an expert by distributing a "how to" list. Compile a list of guidelines to help others make money, save money and time, or make the best use of your products and services. Distribute the information by way of a Web-page column, articles, speeches, handouts, or even salable laminated cards or sheets.

Whether you hand out the information at no cost or sell it, it will position you as an authority and serve as an excellent marketing piece.

Get your name out by speaking to groups whose members you seek to influence. Finally, get your name out by developing a high profile in your industry in other ways. Become active in your trade group, association, or community. Direct activities, lead drives, coordinate events, chair panels, facilitate roundtables, and conduct and publish surveys within your area of expertise.

Help others. Become a mentor, offer your services and resources to junior members of your profession, speak out and write about what's worked for you—and what hasn't. Convene and participate in an "Ask the Experts" panel for your trade association, or volunteer at a local Career Day.

Selling yourself as an expert involves becoming a resource in your field, a clearinghouse of information.

Use Resources

As a resource, familiarize yourself with the resources available to you. The local library is a treasure trove of resources, ranging from databases and reference materials to periodicals and association directories.

Consider all the library information sources available to you. For example, if you want to expand your knowledge and expertise about companies in your industry, your library may have on file the annual reports of these companies. These can enlighten you about their clients, product lines, growth strategies, marketing plans, and more. You may be able to obtain some of the same information by checking out the Web pages of these firms.

For more insights about these companies, check your library for sources such as:

- *Applied Science & Technology Index*
- Bacon's newspaper and magazine directories
- *Business Periodicals Index*
- *Directory of Associations*
- *Hendrick's Commercial Register of the United States*
- *Million Dollar Directory* (Dun & Bradstreet)
- *Moody's Industrial Manual*
- *Standard & Poor's Register of Corporations, Directors and Executives*
- *Thomas Register of American Manufacturers*

(Also see Tip #118 for more resources.)

Share Resources

As a recognized expert in your field, you'll want to develop your own resource library—or at least an extensive bibliography of available resources. Put together a source list and include yourself on it.

Get yourself listed in your industry's directories, both in print and online. Regularly refer others to your

Web page, and provide ample background information about your industry on your page.

Offer free information—pamphlets, laminated cards, "white paper" reports, booklets, and more—that will enlighten others and enhance your image as an expert.

Take on the responsibility of getting answers to questions—any questions—about your profession or department. It's the price you have to pay for the many advantages of marketing yourself as an expert.

But it certainly isn't a very high price. When you commit to increasing your knowledge in your field, it should be all that much easier to reinforce the impression that you are an expert.

Specialization

This is not to say that you nor any other "expert" should claim to know everything there is to know about your industry. But there are areas in which you are more experienced and skilled. You are more than just an expert, you are a specialist.

Ask most sales reps or entrepreneurs who they try to reach, and all too often "anyone" is the reply. "Anyone" makes for a poor target, since you don't know who "anyone" is. There's no way of knowing what organizations that "anyone" belongs to, nor which publications "anyone" reads. You can't share you expertise with "anyone." You can't promote yourself to just "anyone."

Focus

Promote those areas in which you specialize. Like the real estate agent who sells himself as a specialist in mountain properties and vacation homes. And the account manager for an air purification company who bills herself as a specialist with high-tech firms. And the owner of a business office security company, a self-described specialist in downtown high-rise buildings.

A good rule of thumb for self-promoters is: the narrower the niche the better. You don't need to come across as an expert to everyone, nor can you. All that matters is that you are perceived as an expert in your industry. Make it your goal to become an expert—the biggest name in floor coverings, or stocks and bonds, or college athlete recruitment.

That rule of thumb doesn't apply to major corporations. McDonald's can get away with identifying its niche as "families." Pepsi Cola can aim its marketing at "the middle class." Apple Computer can aim for "small and professional users." Hyatt Legal Services can target "working-class Americans."

As individuals, however, we need a sharper focus. We head our own personal corporations, and need to zero in on a narrower field.

You can position yourself within your niche by elaborating on the benefits you offer. Remember that those you seek to influence within that niche want to know what you can do for them. It's a good idea to tune into that "radio" station your audience listens to—WII-FM ("What's In It For Me?")—as you create your list of 10 or more benefits. (See also Chapter 1.)

Targeting a unique niche can pay off big. Publisher Arthur Schiff ventured where others dared not, seeking to sell copies of his *City Family* magazine to new immigrants and others lacking the skills to read English. While other New York publishers pursued upscale demographics, Schiff discovered that up to a half of his readers were eligible for Medicaid,

Pizza Anyone?

For Amir Jahanarai, hospital night staffs turned out to be a profitable niche.

Jahanarai, whose story was recounted in *Success* magazine, was a penniless Iranian immigrant who went to work for $200 a week at his uncle's pizzeria in Joliet, Illinois. While throwing away leftover pizzas one night, Jahanarai got the idea to approach hospitals after hours.

Jahanarai "took to roaming the floors with stacks of steaming hot pies, asking the nurses if they had ordered pizza. No one had. But the aroma sold 10 pies a night," according to the magazine.

Eventually Jahanarai took over the store, and within a year transformed the company from $2500 in weekly sales to $17,000. By defining his niche, Jahanarai laid the groundwork for his future success.

Beat 'Em to the Punch

Timing is important when creating your image as an expert in your market. Writing in *Entrepreneur* magazine, marketing gurus Jack Trout and Al Ries note that "it's better to be first than to be better." They point out how such companies as Federal Express, Krazy Glue, Gore-Tex, and Jeep rode their "early bird" market presence to rise to the tops of their markets.

making their incomes only about $15,000 a year.

Within two years, *City Family's* circulation jumped from 10,000 to 200,000, and ad revenue climbed from zero (the first ads were free) to $60,000 per issue—thanks to increased advertising by companies such as Eastman Kodak. *Library Journal* named the publication one of the ten best new magazines of 1993.

Dealing With Change

No matter what your specialty and area of expertise, be prepared to adapt them to changing times and circumstances. Be flexible about how and where you use your expertise.

"Just when you think you've graduated from the school of hard knocks, someone thinks up a new course."
—Anonymous

Caroline Clarke, in a recent article in *Black Enterprise* magazine, stressed the importance of being "willing—and prepared— to reinvent yourself again and again."

What that involves, she said, is transferring your skills when the need arises, perhaps "from a dying industry to a growing one, from a big-but-rocky company to a small, stable one."

Help the Media Promote You

As you think about establishing your image as an expert, think big. Understand that your best results will come when you share your expertise with the widest possible audience. To do this, you need the media's help.

The good news is that the media needs your help as well. Reporters, editors, and producers rely heavily on sources to help them do their job. Sources provide them with the ideas, tips, and leads that assist them in covering their beats—and, in some cases, their rear ends.

Your goal, as a "self" salesperson, is to become that source. Cultivate media relationships by supplying reporters with the information they need today, or may need tomorrow. Skilled self-promoters provide the answers before reporters pose the questions. Often those reporters will create their questions based on the "answers" supplied earlier by their sources.

What we have here, then, is a symbiotic relationship between you, as the source, and the media. You need them to help you widely promote your expertise. They need you to keep them current on your area of expertise.

Sharing your information with local and trade media will increase the likelihood they will call on you for future interviews on your topic. The more tips and trends you supply the media, the more you solidify your image as an expert in the know.

Begin compiling your media mailing and contact list, if you haven't done so already. (For more on publicity, see Chapter 6.)

Positioning Yourself with Your Market

What matters is that the right people know and appreciate you. Ask yourself who needs to be familiar with you in order for you to achieve your goals. Make a list of the business owners, executives, buyers, purchasing agents, chief financial officers, committee chair persons, officers, and other decision makers who you need to know—and who need to know about you.

Determine if anyone on that list knows you by name. If not, why not? What would it take for you do to become known to those individuals?

Marketing yourself effectively means targeting your audience; targeting your audience means identifying and getting to know "your public."

Understanding Your Audience

You will be most effective in promoting yourself when you have the clearest possible picture of your target audience. Try to change places with members of that audience, in keeping with the sales philosophy that "to sell Harry Smith what Harry Smith buys, you have to see the world through Harry Smith's eyes."

Ponder the perceptions of your public. What do they think of your profession and industry? More importantly, what do they think of you?

Identify their pain, and try to comprehend what hurts them when they deal with the products or services you offer, or the industry in which you are involved.

Be a Consultant

Why not add "consultant" to your list of job titles and qualifications? If you have expertise, and the ability to relate it to an individual's needs, you have what it takes to consult in your field of interest.

It's not quite that easy to launch a consulting career, of course. But the market might be there. When professionals contact you about an article you wrote or a speech you delivered, they likely will inquire about how your information relates to their situation. That's when you can offer your paid consulting services.

Stretch Yourself

As with other strenuous activity, establishing your expertise requires some stretching beforehand.

The stretching I refer to here is the kind that involves accentuating the positive about yourself to the highest degree, and placing yourself in the best possible light. (You may have experienced that stretching sensation in creating your commercial in Chapter 2.)

To achieve public recognition as an expert in your field, you must first act and look the part. It helps to exude the confidence of the "arriver," rather than the uncertainty of the "striver," and to convey the impression that you *already are* the master in your field that others strive to be.

Fake It 'til You Make It

To some, this idea of saying that you are something that—for the moment at least—you aren't, is a sham. An outrage!

But it is nothing more than appreciating and giving yourself credit for your capabilities, and recognizing the subjective nature of the words "expert," and "master," and "success." There are no formal criteria to meet in order to earn those titles. Now is as good a time as any to promote your expertise and success.

Of Self-Esteem, Self-Respect, and Pride

The most important single quality of success and happiness is a positive mental attitude, a general feeling of optimism about yourself and your future.

There are four universal principles, or laws, that determine your levels of self-esteem, self-respect, and personal pride.

1. Law of Belief. Your beliefs become your realities. Biggest single challenge? Self-limiting beliefs.

2. Law of Expectations. Whatever you expect, with confidence, becomes your own "self-fulfilling prophecy."

3. Law of Attraction. You are a "living magnet." You attract into your life people and circumstances in harmony with your dominant thoughts.

4. Law of Correspondence. Your outer world is a mirror of your inner world.

There are three key ideas that explain your levels of self-esteem, self-respect, and personal pride:

1. All causation is mental.

2. You become what you think about most of the time.

3. If you change your thinking, you change your life.

—Brian Tracy

To finish your education in "Establishing Your Expertise," I've taken the liberty of enrolling you in a school. It's a very special school—one attended by some of the world's most prominent and successful self-promoters.

It's called the "Fake It 'til You Make It School."

Now that you're enrolled, there are a few things you should know about the Fake It 'til You Make It School. First, some words on what it isn't. It isn't an educational facility that offers courses in advanced calculus or Greco-Roman philosophy or psychiatry. It doesn't have a campus or a football team.

What it is: an institution dedicated to helping you convert your vision into reality.

The school's curricula is designed to help you:

Act Like an Expert

Communicate how valuable your time is and how busy you are. Schedule appointments with such comments as, "If the afternoon is not good for you, I can change my other appointment and see you in the morning," or "I need to be in your area next week. How would Tuesday do?" or "I have lunch open tomorrow—does that work for you?"

Accentuate...your assets
Exaggerate...your mission (i.e., think big)
Eliminate...self-doubt
Graduate...with a degree in "arriving" rather than "striving."

There's no final exam nor graduation ceremony at the "Fake It 'til You Make It" school. Rather, you'll *know* when you have completed your course of study there. It will be the day when you feel comfortable telling others—and yourself—that you *already are* successful.

You *already are* an expert. You simply need to package and promote your expertise in a way that the right people will notice.

Action Ideas and Tips

101 **Call yourself an expert.** If you don't, others won't either.
Make sure you include the "e-word" in your marketing materials and in the information you provide to those who introduce you. Put it in your "about the author" paragraph that follows an article that you write.

102 **Be concise with your commercial.** Condense your message down to the simplest terms, so that you can communicate your specialty in the fewest words possible.
Practice until you can define your expertise in a single sentence.

103 **Be a believer.** Experts say what they believe, and believe what they say. Present your topic and yourself with passion and enthusiasm.
That will convince others of your conviction and your expertise.

104 **Are you a "household name"?**
Try this test. List the 50 organizations and individuals that you most seek to influence, and determine how many of them consider you a household name.
That should give you an idea of how much additional visibility you need—and how much more self-promotion it will take.

105 **Ask lots of questions.** To promote yourself as an expert, you need to know what you're talking about. And you need to keep current on your topic.
You can never have too much information, nor ask too many questions. Your questions will stimulate your thinking—and prove to others your commitment to stay up-to-date on your information.

106 **Listen to the answers.** The most enlightened experts— and the best salespeople—are the best listeners.
You'll earn the respect of others by doing the most listening, not the most talking. When you concentrate on what others say, you can be more effective in how you respond. That, in turn, will reinforce your image as a knowledgeable individual.

107 **Invite input, but go with your gut.** Solicit advice and welcome opinions, but understand that ultimately yours is the only opinion that matters.
Automatically following popular policies won't establish you as an expert. Forming and following your own policies will.
Be grateful for others' advice, but be partial to your own.

108 Talk about what you know, learn about what you don't.
Speaking out on issues you know nothing about will damage your credibility. Stick to the topics with which you're familiar, and educate yourself about the other ones. When you don't know something, admit it.

109 Run, don't walk, to come up with the answers you don't have. Even as an expert, you're not expected to have all the answers. But you're expected to get them.

Don't let the sun set on an unanswered question. Waste no time in tracking down the answers—and sharing progress reports with the individual who posed the question.

110 Pause to ponder. Don't feel compelled to respond immediately to tough questions. Reflect on your response.

There's power in the pause. Don't think others will doubt your expertise if you don't have ready responses to every query. The most knowledgeable individuals take time to carefully consider difficult questions before offering answers.

111 Conquer comparisons. Comparisons are inevitable when you take over a good territory from a leading salesperson.

Some ways to handle questions about why you do things differently:
- Keep your cool. Understand that time—and your success—will put an end to the comments from the peanut gallery. But

keep your ears and your mind open; you may want to adopt some of the strategies practiced by your predecessor.
- Develop your own style. Discuss your goals with those you seek to influence. Your skill in achieving those goals will silence your critics.
- Go with your strengths. Spend your time and energy building on your assets, rather than trying to duplicate those of your predecessor.
- Be confident. Remind others of your past success doing things "your way."

—Increasing Your Sales Success
by Thomas Quick

112 Keep an assist list. Keep a roster of everyone...everyone you help. That goes for clients, colleagues, associates, protégés and others.

Maintain a database of all those you serve, with details about how you serve them. You can use that information to prove the breadth of your experience—and the extent of your expertise.

113 Use the success of others to validate your own.
Create a scrapbook of client success stories, documenting the many ways that others have benefited from your services. Include testimonial letters—or, simply, comments they share with you by phone or e-mail. Update your information by calling former clients regularly to check on their progress.

114 Drop names. Bring a list of your high-profile clients to net-working events. Adapt your list for each event, choosing the names that will have the most impact on those you meet.

Draw from a similar list when you're creating cover letters or other marketing materials, again adapting the names to your audience.

115 Share your "how to's." Create a list of tips that others can use to make or save money, save time, make the most of your services, or otherwise improve their lives. Print the information on a handout sheet or a laminated card for distribution along with your business card.

116 Turn your "how to's" into special reports. Convert your tips into one- and two-page reports. Use the reports as marketing pieces, frequent-buyer awards, or a value-added element for your customers.

Or provide them, along with a cover letter, to the media or others you seek to influence.

117 Audiotape your expertise. Record your tips, insights and strategies, and send audiocassettes to those you seek to influence.

You should have a captive audience, considering how much time people spend listening to audio cassettes while commuting. Inform your listeners about how and where to contact you.

118 Build a resource list. Compile a mailing list of all the trade publications in your field, and the national media that might be interested in your expertise. Consult such resources as:

- *Oxbridge Directory of Newsletters*
- *Hudson Directory of Newsletters*
- *Gale Directory of Publications*
- *Gale Directories in Print*
- *Working Press of the Nation*
- *Newsletters in Print*
- *Standard Periodical Directory*

When you contact media outlets, provide a media kit which includes key industry information, questions often asked about your industry, industry clients, and other pertinent data.

119 Compile a mailing list of local media. Consult your library for a reference guide to local print and broadcast outlets.

Try to arrange for local appointments, if possible, and make available the same information described in tip #118.

120 Build relationships with reporters and editors. Meet with reporters and editors of trade and general media outlets, and offer yourself as a future interviewee and news source. Find out what their information needs are, and offer to help meet those needs in any way you can.

121 Plan monthly contacts. Use e-mail, fax, and regular mail to keep in touch with your media list. Update them regularly on new developments in your field, along with sources of information on those developments. Provide them with a steady flow of story ideas and timely topics, along with news clippings and other background information.

122 **Ask for help.** Contact your top references for their help in creating or enhancing your image as an expert. Provide them with your "expert" credentials and ask that they share that information with any one who calls with questions about your qualifications.

123 **Help others.** Helping others can help enhance your image as an expert.

Offer to write testimonial and reference letters for others, or to create endorsements for their products. Your efforts will provide you with visibility and name recognition.

124 **Promote yourself as a consultant.** You position yourself as an expert by offering to share your knowledge with individuals or organizations. Promote your consultation service through articles, private communication, speeches and other methods.

125 **Give to charities.** Contribute your consulting time or other professional service to a charity event.

Select those causes that appeal to you most, and be generous with your time and support. Distribute copies of promotional material citing your involvement in the event.

126 **Create a course.** Draw from your expertise to develop a course that you can offer at a community college, adult education center or elsewhere. Promote the fact that you have developed the course, and contact area institutions about promoting it, and you, in their catalogs.

127 **Turn your class into a media event.** If you get the opportunity to teach your course, contact the media with details about it. Include information on key issues it addresses, the material it covers and the students it attracts. Invite reporters to attend.

128 **Hit the books.** Brush up and stay up on your area of expertise by reading, and by enrolling in seminars offered through your company, your trade organization, or a local college. Select advanced courses that will keep you current on the latest technology. List the courses on your Web page, in your one-sheet, and in your other marketing materials.

129 **Work with a mentor.** Seek out a prominent member of your industry who is willing to share his or her expertise with you. In return, offer any kind of assistance that they or you deem appropriate.

However knowledgeable you are, you can expand your knowledge by studying under a mentor.

130 **Master market research.** Some sources for that research:

- your own questionnaires
- data banks accessible via computer modem and phone
- chambers of commerce market studies
- associations and trade groups within your industry
- publications that serve your industry, and their market studies
- University Microfilms (800-521-0600), which has access to over one million PhD dissertations

—*Guerrilla Marketing Weapons* by Jay Conrad Levinson

131 **Spotlight the stars.** Approach the most prosperous professionals in your field with a request to interview them for a possible trade publication article.

That will gain you access to those you don't know, and will enable you to gain valuable insights that you can apply to your own career.

If the article gets published, they'll be grateful. If it doesn't get published, they'll be flattered that you tried.

132 **Use a newsletter to maintain your expert image.** Whether you send it out electronically or by mail, your expert's newsletter should have a different spin than the typical self-marketing newsletter. It should emphasize advice, tips, and information, rather than your products and services.

133 **Keep yourself—and your expertise—in front of your customers.** Staying in touch with a buyer after a sale is more than just smart customer service. It's a good way to retain your image as an expert.

Call after the sale with advice on how best to use the product, and your customer will admire your continued interest—and respect your know-how.

134 **Answer questions.** They have questions, you have answers. The addition of an "Ask the Expert" feature to your Web site will increase interest in it—and you. Launch it by printing and responding to often-asked questions. Keep the information interesting and timely, and, before long, visitors will send in their own questions.

135 **Get listed.** Keep an eye out for reference lists accompanying articles in your area of expertise. If a list doesn't include your name and resources, suggest that the writer or editor add them.

136 **Become an information clearinghouse.** Assemble what people need to know about your area of expertise, and make it available to others. Develop a reputation as THE expert to whom others turn for sources, contacts, articles, and other background about your field.

137 **Create an industry-information "care package."** Include historical notes, pertinent facts, key issues, a list of key players, background information about yourself and other material that outsiders would find useful.

Promoting and distributing the kit can only bolster your image as an expert.

138 **Arrive well before a meeting—and linger after.** By showing up several minutes before a sales meeting or presentation and sticking around after it ends, you demonstrate your willingness to learn. Experts are good at that.

The extra mingling time also gives you an opportunity to share your expertise in an informal, one-on-one way.

139 **Beware of the credibility killers!** Steer clear of phrases that weaken the impact of your words. Some examples:

- "I think..."
- "It's only my opinion..."
- "I may be wrong, but..."
- "You might want to think about this..."
- "This may or may not be true, but..."
- "Take this for what it's worth..."
- "I have a silly question..."
- "You may not believe this, but..."
- "To be honest with you..."
- "I'm sorry..."

140 **Watch your but(s).** Avoid the "B-word" when its use comes across as an excuse (e.g., "My sales would have been better, but the winter was especially cold"). Using the word "and" adds a more positive spin

("It was a challenging year, and I learned how cold weather can affect your sales").

141 **Know your competitors better than they know themselves.** Do what you have to do to become an expert on what they offer as well as what you do. Review their Web pages and marketing materials, memorize their price lists, check out their annual reports, interview their clients and suppliers—whatever it takes.

That will prepare you for "comparison shoppers" and demonstrate your command of your industry.

142 **Stay connected.** From *Fortune* magazine editor Marshall Loeb comes this advice: "Become known in your industry. Build a list of 25 competitors, suppliers, stock analysts, management consultants and former colleagues and call them every 3-6 months."

143 **Climb the association ladder.** The sooner you get involved in your trade group or association, the sooner your name will be known.

Getting involved means serving on committees, contributing articles to the group's publication, speaking at conferences, running for the board, and otherwise volunteering your services wherever and however you can.

The payback: You'll connect with some key industry players—and gain a reputation as a player, yourself.

144 **When you can't talk about work, talk about activities.**

Compensate for your lack of work experience in an area by discussing your activities in that area. Those activities suggest you have expertise.

Say, for example, you bid on a contract that requires some financial analysis—and you have no job experience in that area. You could, however, mention your responsibility managing money as treasurer for a local fundraising drive.

145 Lock the door on the skeletons in the closet. Don't let yesterday's mistakes derail your efforts to establish yourself as an expert.

Don't discuss past errors or setbacks unless asked about them. Refer to the lessons learned, and how the experiences added to your understanding. The best way to overcome a negative reputation is to begin work on a positive one, by creating and sharing your expertise.

146 Talk up your profession. Job fairs, school career days, industry job-opportunity events—all offer opportunities to discuss your career and your success. Your participation will increase your exposure and image as an expert.

147 Hang your plaques. If you've got 'em, show 'em. Certificates, degrees, awards—all of them can dress up your office wall and showcase your experience.

Include them as part of your "Wall of Fame" along with framed copies of your best testimonial letters. They will speak for themselves—and say a lot about you.

148 Get the picture. When you work with or get to know key figures within your industry, or celebrities in general, have your picture taken. An image of the two of you side by side is one of those pictures that will say a thousand words.

149 Use your degrees. Your academic titles may give you a competitive edge when you're making a sale—or an impression.

Include yours in your personal marketing materials and cite them in appropriate conversations.

150 Write a book. Nothing positions you better as an expert.

CHAPTER FOUR

Million-Dollar Marketing on a Shoestring Budget

"Life is short, and so is money."
—Bertolt Brecht, *The Threepenny Opera*

Some of the best personal promotion you can do is the kind you don't pay for. Sales professionals, entrepreneurs, franchisees, and others can effectively promote themselves and make a major impact for a minimal investment of time and money.

Once you decide on your message and to whom you want to appeal, reaching your audience can be quite economical. Free publicity and public speaking are among the dozens of low-cost, no-cost promotional options available to you.

You can take the price out of promotion if you ignore all of the "ya gottas" for marketing success from some of those self-proclaimed experts out there.

I'm talking about the gurus and consultants who insist that "ya gotta" have a state-of-the-art brochure—four-color, of course—complete with glossy photographs and fancy fonts. And that "ya gotta" hire a graphic designer to create a futuristic Web site for you. And that "ya gotta" invest in full-page advertisements in major publications.

Effective Marketing Doesn't Have to Break the Bank

It's as if those marketing gurus are convinced that you have to be rich before you can get recognized.

Don't believe it. Don't fall for that conventional—and misguided—wisdom that marketing is expensive. Yes, it can be. But it doesn't have to be.

Nor is there any truth to those age-old theories that a significant percentage of your company's gross profits *must* be reinvested in marketing, that promotion is complicated and time-consuming, and that all organizations should hire a marketing director.

Baloney! When it comes to marketing, bigger is not necessarily better. What matters is not what you spend on promoting yourself and your organization. What matters is that you do it differently—and "differently" can be done economically.

A powerful personal commercial may be all you need to stand out from your competitors—even those competitors with much deeper pockets than yours. The face-to-face impression you make is more meaningful than another person's fancy Web page, pricey video, or slick ad campaign.

Your gifts of gab and self-promotion can be worth more than another company's big marketing budget.

Use your negotiating skills to save on marketing costs. Negotiate for everything: printing, advertising, services from your Internet provider.

Use your communications skills to reach out to others. Avoid costly mistakes by consulting with mentors and focus groups.

There's no limit to the amount of money an individual or company *could* spend on marketing, of course. But the cost of your marketing materials matters less than their timeliness, relevance, applicability, uniqueness, and lasting appeal.

The Value of Planning

More important than your personal marketing budget is your marketing *focus*. Someone with a good marketing plan is destined for greater success than a person with expensive materials but not much else.

Self-promoters without a plan are like ships without rudders; they may have a vague idea where they want to go, but not the faintest idea on how to get there. The plan need not be a multipage epic, nor read like the Great American Novel. A simple page will do, summarizing your message, your market, and the methods by which you want to reach it.

Does Advertising Really Work?

By 1996, the U.S. spent $11.5 billion on advertising—BIG money, considering the impact, or lack thereof, of that investment. A study by Yankelovich Partners and Gannett's *USA Weekend* magazine of 1,000 consumers nationwide showed that only 25 percent of them said a television ad would induce them to try a new product or brand.

Only 15 percent said they would be motivated to purchase by a newspaper ad, and only 13 percent by a magazine ad. A mere three percent reported they would be influenced by the endorsement—in any media—by a celebrity.

As popular as infomercials have become since the deregulation of the television industry in the mid-1980s, their success rate is spotty. Industry experts estimate that, of all the products promoted via infomercials, only one in 20 makes a hit.

Observed Hal Quinley, a partner at Yankelovich: "Advertising has little confidence among consumers. It ranks below the federal government."

"I know half my advertising is wasted. I just don't know which half."
—John Wanamaker,
department store owner

Opportunities Abound

Talk shows are looking for guests. Public access channels are looking for hosts. Trade schools and vocational training centers are looking for teachers.

Trade groups in your field are looking for volunteers. Professionals in related fields are looking for joint promotion opportunities.

It takes time to get published, get speaking engagements, get interviewed on a show or host your own, become active in trade groups, and network with allied professionals. But these activities don't take much money.

Consider all of the opportunities for you to take the

"price" out of your promotion. Editors of publications in your field and outside it are looking for articles, letters to the editor, commentaries and columns. Organizations are looking for speakers. Many outlets want to hear what you have to say, and won't charge you to say it. In some cases, they may *pay* you to say it.

Teach a Class

One of the many options available to the cost-conscious personal promoter is teaching a continuing education course. Approach your local adult education center with the idea of sharing your expertise in a class.

First, the bad news: Your pay will be paltry and your class attendance may be sparse. It's rare when an adult education class draws more than 15 attendees.

So, why bother?

You bother because of the catalog. Chances are that the program catalog will be distributed to thousands of local homes and businesses, frequently to every residence in the area. That means free area-wide distribution of your name, information about your course, and your credentials. And that means a great deal of visibility and credibility for you.

What do people assume when they see your name affiliated with a course in a catalog? That you're the *authority* on that subject, of course. And, that you'll likely have the answers to their questions on the subject.

The result: business for you from individuals who might not have the slightest intention of attending your class.

	Ideas for Courses
Accountant	Accounting for the small business owner
Contractor	How to winter-proof your home
Financial planner	Protecting retirement and windfall assets
Insurance agent	Long-term care insurance: The pros and cons
Interior designer	Kitchen design
Landscaper	Low-maintenance landscaping
Photographer	Using a point-and-shoot camera to take great pictures
Psychologist	Self-esteem in the workplace
Real estate agent	What every home buyer needs to know

Offer a course in real estate, for example, and people may call you when they're looking to buy a new home or to sell theirs. Teach a retirement planning class, and you may hear from investors looking to buy mutual funds. Present a program on creating a Web page, and you may get some orders from prospects who want you to develop theirs.

Stories abound of key contacts and fat contracts resulting from course write-ups in adult education catalogs.

Before approaching a continuing education center with *your* course, review the box to the left.

Teach 'Em and Reach 'Em

Use this 10-point checklist to plan your adult education course:

(1) Who to reach?

(2) What to tell them?

(3) What to call your course?

(4) How to describe it?

(5) How to describe yourself?

(6) Where to teach it?

(7) How to "sell" it?

(8) How to present it?

(9) How to promote it?

(10) How to follow up?

More Low-Cost Promotions

Personal Networking

Polish your networking skills and you'll economize on your marketing. You'll read more about networking in Chapter 7, but the key point here is that it will save you money if you make your "net" work.

Individuals in your personal network can help you make a significant marketing impact for little or no cost. Those with whom you network can serve you in any number of ways.

People in your network can be scouts on the lookout for hot leads and business opportunities for you, and for information about your competitors. They can be couriers, communicating your message and other information about your services to those they know—and those you *should* know. They can be your promoters and public relations representatives.

Then, too, your networking contacts can serve as your board of advisors—your "sounding board" for new initiatives. Some may qualify as mentors. Others may even turn out to be part-time account managers and sales reps who actually bring in business for you.

Donate Your Time

When it comes to marketing yourself, time is a critical resource: You want to make the most of it. That's why you have to be choosy when you consider whether to *donate* your time.

If your motives are strictly benevolent—and you're to be commended if they are—then give your time based on strictly charitable considerations. That is, determine how you want to give based on the causes you feel are most worthy. The end result: spiritual fulfillment.

If, on the other hand, your motives are based on personal marketing considerations, evaluate those causes differently. Get involved only with those charitable events that will give you the greatest amount of visibility in the shortest amount of time. The end result: financial fulfillment.

If personal promotion is your only goal, be careful. Donating your time and services for that purpose can be a mixed blessing. Done correctly, it can provide you with the exposure that makes you money. Done incorrectly, it can waste your time and thereby *cost* you money.

From the self-promotion standpoint, a key advantage of donating your time to charitable groups is that they do the marketing for you. They will publicize you in their promotional materials and advertising. That's true whether you contribute your products to a charity auction or donate a few hours of your consulting time.

Often the sponsoring group publicizes the event by creating materials that may be worthy additions to your own promotion portfolio. Hold on to any material—from program flyers to local articles—that mentions your involvement.

Your involvement in a charitable event can generate goodwill and good name recognition.

It can also provide a good boost to your career if your participation promotes your expertise. Contributing your knowledge will reap you more public relations benefits than participating in a walkathon or volunteering at a soup kitchen. Publicity

> "Goodwill is the one and only asset that competition cannot undersell or destroy."
> —Marshall Field

resulting from the fact that you donated your consultation time bolsters your image as an expert.

Similarly, there is more PR value in donating your own products to a worthy cause than in providing items unrelated to your business. It makes more sense in a charity auction for a telecommunications equipment provider to donate a pager than two free passes to a rock concert.

Descriptions of the products and services that you donate add to the understanding people have of what you do and why you're special.

It's important that you attach a value to the time and commodities that you contribute to charitable causes. One way is to include an itemized invoice, with the words "professional courtesy" printed across the front. That enables you to maintain financial integrity and assures that others won't assume you'll give away your services in the future.

There may be considerable return on the investment of time that you donate to charity. You can gain visibility and credibility, marketing pieces, a good public image and an edge over your competitors who *don't* get involved in worthy causes.

More Ways to Save

Include promotional information in your invoices and statements. That assures widespread exposure for that information, since several decision makers often review those invoices prior to their approval.

Reduce your phone bills by sending e-mail messages rather than calling. When possible, transmit information by e-mail and fax rather than through the mail. You can distribute hundreds of e-mail messages for the cost of a few stamps.

Send faxes over the Internet and save up to 80 percent over conventional point-to-point phone connections. Advertise your Web site without paying to do so by joining a link exchange. Place banner ads of other exchange members on your site, and other members will run yours.

Turn your newsletters and flyers into self-mailers. Conduct business meetings over breakfast. Restrict your long-distance calls and fax transmissions to off-hours.

If you're used to paying top dollar for print and broadcast advertising, you might question the principle of money-saving marketing.

Before you invest further in advertising, compare the impact of those ads against stories that might appear in print or on the air about your company. Clearly, news accounts about you and your organization carry far more credibility than your ads. Your prospects are more likely to believe positive information about you if the media, rather than you, provide it.

The way David Ogilvy sees it, your prospects are much more likely to *notice* an article than an advertisement. Ogilvy, author of the book *Confessions of an Advertising Man*, estimates that "roughly six times as many people read the average article as the average advertisement."

"That's because people are more interested in information than in fluff—the latter being what most ads are full of," Ogilvy says.

Advertising considerations should be based on "return" as well as credibility issues. How much return do you get on an advertising campaign?

Punch Up Your Marketing Materials

You don't have to invest in new marketing materials to make the personal sale. Add more promotional punch to the materials you use now. Add a personal blurb on that cover sheet you send out with your faxes. Print information about yourself on your invoice forms. Include similar information on the back of your business cards.

Even if your marketing budget is tight, put together at least one promotional piece that will tell your unique, personal story. This could be a personal one-sheet (see Chapter 5) or it could be an article or testimonial letter. Each can have lasting

NAKARA MAINTENANCE SERVICE

The only service that offers "all natural" cleaning products.

FAX

TRANSMISSION

To: _____

From: _____

We care for your office.

influence and can enhance your image as an expert, showcase your talents, and position you within a niche or industry.

Direct Marketing

Direct marketing doesn't come cheaply, according to *The Direct Marketer.* Sending 10,000 pieces of direct mail may cost you $1 each. Telemarketing carries a price tag of $3-5 per call.

Promotional videos became the marketing toy of choice for a number of groups in the early 1990s. Ski resorts, financial institutions, farm tractor manufacturers, and supermarkets were among the organizations that spent a minimum of $30,000 to create videos for target markets. Car companies routinely shelled out $1 million to produce a single video. Some 14 million of these direct marketing videos were distributed in 1994.

Frequency Counts

How often you send something to your target audience can be as important as *what* you send. Monthly mail-outs of a single article by or about you, or a single testimonial letter, may be more effective than sending out a marketing kit that will get stashed—or, worse yet, trashed.

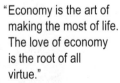

"Economy is the art of making the most of life. The love of economy is the root of all virtue."
—George Bernard Shaw

Don't Use the Latest, Use the Most Effective

You could—and so many individuals do—shell out every spare dollar for the latest and greatest marketing technology and tools with all the bells and whistles.

No matter how much you invest in computer marketing software, there are more programs out there that someone, somewhere will tell you that you need. But it can be far more sensible—and economical—to make better use of what you have.

Software manufacturers are always coming up with newer and fancier ways to develop a personal newsletter. But before you rush to your favorite software store, review your current operating system. You may find that the program it contains for newsletter production—such as Microsoft Publisher—may more than meet your needs, once you take full advantage of it.

Similarly, you can invest in costly phone answering services and systems to assure that callers will get a timely response. Or you can upgrade your current system simply by changing the voice mail message daily.

Trade Show Tricks

Companies, large and small, spend big bucks on trade shows to show off their latest and greatest state-of-the-art equipment to anyone who is interested—and to many who are not. The problem with trade show exhibiting is twofold: It's expensive and it's passive. It's marketing that works only if prospects come to you.

An economical and *proactive* alternative is to work the trade show floor by networking among the multitudes. By scaling down your exhibit, you can free your staff to network and distribute marketing materials on the floor.

Business for my Washington news bureau increased dramatically once I stopped exhibiting—and started roving—at the Radio-TV News Directors Association conferences. I would collect 50 or more cards from news directors at each event by circulating freely. I doubt if 50 people even walked by my booth the year that I paid the price for a conventional booth.

Market Smarter, Not Harder

Wise professionals realize that marketing, alone, doesn't yield the kind of results that *smart* marketing does. Smart marketing is anything you do to make a maximum marketing impact for a minimal investment of time and money.

Lining up appearances on TV or radio talk shows is smart marketing. So is networking. So is teaching an adult education class. So is any other strategy that affords you a great deal of exposure for not much money.

Joe Sabah discovered that he could practice and profit from smart marketing without ever leaving home. Sabah, a Denver-based speaker and co-author of the book *How to Get the Job You Really Want and Get Employers to Call You*, sought alternative ways to promote his book when he discovered that bookstores and distributors take over three months to pay authors' invoices.

A brief stint on a Denver station convinced him that radio talk shows would provide him with outstanding opportunities to sell books without stepping outside his front door.

Sabah discovered that there are over 700 radio talk shows on the lookout for interview guests. He subsequently appeared on more than 600 of these shows, selling a whopping $367,000 worth of books. That comes to more than 22,750 copies!

"It's as much fun today as it was the first time," Sabah says. "Many times I'm interviewed while I'm in my bathrobe."

> **Get Booked**
>
> Sabah shares his tricks of the trade in another book, entitled *How to Get on Radio Talk Shows All Across America Without Leaving Your Home or Office*. For more information and a free report, contact him by phone, 303-722-7200, or e-mail, JSabah@aol.com

Reach Influencers

You can get a powerful return on even a small marketing investment once you stop, look, and listen. Pause and set professional goals. Look for a target audience of individuals you can influence in order to achieve those goals, and listen to their needs.

Articles by or about you in publications read by those you seek to influence can boost your career. So can speaking in front of organizations whose members you want to influence.

Smart marketers realize that both the experts in their field, and their current clients are sources of affordable market research. They understand the wisdom

The Art of Creative Marketing

Many are the legends of the money-saving marketing masters, those parsimonious promoters who, in fact or fiction, outmaneuvered complacent competitors whose pockets were deeper but whose imaginations were not.

Cut It Out

There's the tale of the mom-and-pop barber shop that was holding its own until a Fantastic Sam's franchisee moved into the shopping center across the street. With great fanfare, the Fantastic Sam's hair cuttery erected an enormous billboard announcing that "We do $6 haircuts." In response, mom and pop taped a handwritten sign in their window noting that "We FIX $6 haircuts."

Going Up

Then there's the realtor who focused his marketing efforts on riding office building elevators.

He'd enter the packed elevators on the second floor, immediately turn to his fellow passengers and say: "Good morning! If you're wondering why I called this meeting this morning—like this elevator, the cost of housing and office space in this city is going up, up, up. For those of you looking to save money on your next move, here's my card." And he would pass his cards out to his captive—and very surprised—audience.

Let 'Er Rip

And, I can't leave out the one about the penny-pinching pizza store owner in Denver who wasn't about to let Domino's get him down.

Other small pizza store proprietors became horrified—mortified—when Domino's entered the market and immediately took out a full-page Yellow Pages advertisement.

The penny pincher responded by spending a few dollars on a radio campaign offering a two-for-one pizza deal for anyone who brought in the Domino's ad.

Listeners tore out the Domino's Pizza ads from their Yellow Pages. They asked permission from their neighbors to rip out their Dominos Pizza ads. They tore out Domino's ads from phone booth Yellow Pages directories.

Within months, the story goes, there wasn't a Domino's Pizza ad to be found in Metropolitan Denver.

Skilled self-promoters don't get mad. They get even.

of consulting those who have succeeded before them, and those they serve. The simple phrase "I need your help" can work wonders when it comes to obtaining valuable background information at no cost.

Barter

Producing marketing materials can be a pricey proposition, but there's one excellent way to cut your costs. You may be able to barter for business cards, letterhead, brochures, graphic design, or even telemarketing

Clearly you have to offer something in return that printers, designers, and others perceive they need. Perhaps you can make your consulting services available, or certain products or services.

"If I had my life to live over again, I would elect to be a trader of goods rather than a student of science. I think barter is a noble thing."
—Albert Einstein

I speak with some degree of personal experience in bartering. It is the way I have obtained virtually every marketing piece I distribute. I have negotiated deals with printers and designers in which I've exchanged my personal promotion consultation for cards, one-sheets, and the design of printed materials that I sell at my speeches and through the mail.

Bartering is a practice near and dear to penny-wise self-promoters everywhere. Entrepreneurs have used this system to come up with demonstration videos, newsletters, logos, marketing kits, and numerous other promotional gizmos. The value of bartering goes far beyond marketing products and services, of course. Some wheeler-dealers barter for everything from landscaping to computer software, and from tutoring to hotel accommodations and travel.

There is, of course, no guarantee that you will be able to work out a barter deal—but you can and should always get a deal on the services you *do* end up buying. There are, for example, numerous ways you can cut deals on your printing, such as by negotiating discounts in return for payment terms and buying paper in bulk.

* * * * *

The good news about self-promotion is that you can perform magic in your marketing without spending much money to do it.

Action Ideas and Tips

151 **The message means more than the money.** Memorize this: What you *say* is more important than what you *pay* to say it.

Create an effective commercial for yourself (See Chapter 2), and you need not pay a premium for your promotion. Remember that a strong and focused self-marketing message, effectively presented, will do more for you than pricey materials.

152 **Promote yourself in monthly mailings.** Include self-promotion material in the invoices and statements that you send out each month. Enclose the same material in the checks you send suppliers. Both cases will give you an opportunity to promote yourself for no additional postage.

—*Streetfighting* by Jeff Slutsky

153 **Remind those you serve how well you serve them.**

Communicate regularly with clients and others you serve on the many ways that you benefit them. Include details on how you help them make money, save money, save time, increase their influence, manage their business more productively, etc. Schedule meetings, send notes or e-mail messages, add the information onto invoices—whatever it takes to communicate the value to them of the relationship.

The value to you of doing so? More appreciation by your customers, and a greater likelihood they'll do business with—and refer business to—you in the future.

154 **Don't reinvent the wheel.** Model the self-marketing masters, instead. Ask the leaders in your field or your mentors to provide you with copies of their promotional materials.

Seek permission to use their materials as a model for yours. Should they agree, it will save you marketing money and time, and will provide you with a prototype that works.

155 **Send out flyers.** They contain about half the sales space of a brochure at less than 10 percent of the cost. They give you *more* sales space than a small newspaper display ad, again, at a fraction of the cost.

—*Win-Win Marketing*

156 **Fax or e-mail the appetizers before sending out the main course.** Don't go to the expense of mailing all of your promotional materials until you're sure of the interest on the other end.

Respond to casual inquiries about your services with information you transmit via fax or e-mail. Whet their appetites, but don't give away the main course until you're convinced there is legitimate interest.

The right qualifying questions will help determine who has the need, budget and commitment for what you offer—and who is worth the expense of shipping all of your materials.

157 **In with the new—but keep the old.** Don't discard your marketing materials now that you're promoting yourself online. Add your e-mail and Web addresses onto clear laser-printer labels, and stick them on business cards, brochures, letterhead, and other materials until you're ready to reprint.

158 **Team up.** Work out a deal with a noncompeting business that sells to your same market. Ask the company to include your self-promotional materials with their bills or other regular mailings. Offer it as a "value added" for their customers.

159 **Know the answers before you hear the questions.**
Save marketing money and time simply by preparing powerful responses to the following six questions on the minds of all of your prospects:
• Why should I see *you*?
• Why should I *listen*?
• Why should I *trust* you?
• Why should I take *action*?
• Why should I act *now*?

"Ace" a meeting with a prospect by responding to those key questions, and follow-up marketing may be un-necessary. You may get the business on the spot.
  —25 Common Sales Objections & How to Overcome Them by Bob Taylor

160 **Sell your customers on selling you.** Suggest that they profile you in their promotional material. Point out that it will make them look bigger and better to focus on your relationship and on the ways they have benefited since you began working together.

161 **Sign 'em in—and up.**
Pass around a sign-in sheet each time you give a presentation, and get hold of it when you attend one.

These lists may be ripe with prospects. With good follow-up, you may be able to convert some of those contacts into contracts.

162 **Donate to a good cause—and promote your own.**
Offer to contribute a percentage of your sales to a local charity—and promote the fact in their publication. Consult the organization's marketing department about other ways to publicize the partnership.

It works. One Denver home accessory retailer contributed three percent of its holiday sales to Habitat for Humanity, a charity group that builds homes for low-income families. The cooperative effort was promoted in the group's newsletter, which has a mailing list of 15,000, and the retailer increased business dramatically as a result.

163 **"He ain't heavy, he's my retailer."** Lean on your manufacturers and wholesalers for marketing materials and displays for your store.

Ask for such in-store advertising materials as flyers, literature, and aisle displays.

Get your manufacturer or distributor to foot the bill for ads featuring your products. Promote it as an opportunity for them to connect with *their* customers.

—Marketing Without a Marketing Budget by Craig Rice

164 **Barter for promotional services.** Consider signing up with one of the more than 400 barter networks or brokers nationwide, many of which are listed in the Yellow Pages under "Barter and Trade Exchanges."

165 **Negotiate for promotional services.** Even if you can't work out a barter deal for promotional help, you might be able to get a bargain.

Ask for the best available price from printers, graphic designers, and others. Let them know if their offer is out of your budget range. They may lower their price rather than risk losing your business altogether.

You'll never know if you never ask.

166 **Draw attention to your business card by putting useful information on the back.**

Tips, a calendar, a formula or chart, a map to your office—that kind of information on the flip side of your card motivates people to hold onto it.

The additional printing costs involved are minimal and worth it. Consider the possibilities: accountants can list tax deadlines, travel agents can include frequent flyer club phone numbers, etc.

It's a good way to make your business card memorable without busting your marketing budget.

—The Art of Self Promotion newsletter

167 **Leave 'em with a lead card.** Create cards that spell out what kind of leads and prospects you seek. Distribute them along with your business cards or include the information *on* your business cards.

Lead cards clarify your needs and make it easier for others to look out for your best interests. They're excellent networking and business-building tools.

168 **Get feedback on your foes.** What your advisors, mentors, and colleagues have to say about your *competitors'* products is as important as their input on yours.

Ask about your competitors' product quality, selection, service, etc.—and for advice on how you can surpass what they have to offer. Collect their product samples, annual reports, and other materials so you can get instant feedback from your advisors.

169 **Use postcard power.** Postcards give you plenty of bang for your marketing bucks.

Use them to immediately announce new products, private sales, or special events; distribute coupons; or say thank you—without using an envelope. They're inexpensive to print, cheaper than letters to mail and, as Nicholas Bade points out in his book *Marketing Without Money*, they give your message extra exposure. Everyone who handles the card sees your message.

170 **Cut newsletter costs.**
To reduce your newsletter budget without sacrificing quality:
- Eliminate envelope costs by making your newsletter a self-mailer—or enclose it with other regular mailings.
- Shop around for the best deals on paper, typesetting and printing.
- Ask printers for discounts in exchange for a credit line or a year-long contract.
- Create preprinted sections, like a nameplate shell and inside boilerplate.

171 **Sell advertising in your newsletter.** Solicit ads from companies and groups who would be most interested in reaching your readers.

172 **Cut printing costs.**

- Buy paper in bulk.
- Use floor-stock paper the printer has on hand.
- Produce lighter-weight versions of your materials, allowing you to send them for less to "Class B" prospects.
- Use colored stock to give the look of a second color.

- Avoid costly odd sizes; stick with 81/2″ × 11″ sheets when possible.
- Select your photos from a contact sheet, and have only the beset ones printed.
- Insert your own boxes and rules before sending materials to a printer.
- Avoid "bleeds" (photos, art, etc. that runs off the page) and screens.
- Avoid last-minute changes before sending materials to a printer.
- Never work with the originals when bringing in outside clip art; use only copies.

173 **Play the "shell game" with price and product lists.**
Add a touch of class to price, product, and other time-sensitive information by printing it on shells preprinted in color. Simply leave enough space on the shells to revise the information in the future.

174 **Refresh your records.**
Update your call and mailing lists, and databases regularly. It will save you time and money down the road. Keep up with changes in personnel, addresses and phone numbers. Find out who wants to continue receiving your newsletter or other marketing materials. Use the calls to solicit referrals and testimonials.

175 **Pick a postal person.**
Postal service representatives can advise you on minimizing your mailing costs.

Establish a relationship with a helpful source at your post office, and learn about bulk mail, barcoding, and other cost cutting techniques. Ask to be contacted about any new postal discount plans and cost-cutting opportunities.

176 **Cut Internet deals.** Negotiate for the best price for a sales or publicity program on the Net. It's easy to sweeten the deal on a customized package with the server of your choice. Don't pay any more attention to published prices than you do for advertising rate cards. In both cases, you can work out a better financial arrangement.

177 **Use e-mail to save on the phone.** Long-distance phone tag can be pricey, especially when you're chasing a prospect during normal business hours.

Set up appointments by e-mail. Send a message indicating when you'll call next, or when you'll be in your office to receive a callback.

That will save you time as well as money, and will free up your phone lines.

178 **Be frugal with your faxing.** Cut the cost of faxing by transmitting during off-peak hours and omitting a cover page where possible. Broadcast faxing can be a money saver when you send the same fax to many recipients, and LANFAX technology is economical when your daily fax volume is 50 or more.
—Murray Kauffman, The Kauffman Group

179 **Market yourself electronically.** E-mail messages cost less than phone calls, and you can cut or eliminate printing and postage costs by posting promotional information on your Web page.

Send faxes over the Internet rather than phone lines and lower your faxing costs by as much as 80 percent. New software makes net faxing as easy as clicking a mouse.

180 **Use your Web site for market research.** Ask visitors to your site if they want to be notified of new products and services, and special sales. It costs you little, and will save you money in the long run, if you gather the names and addresses of interested parties by e-mail.

181 **Use your Web site for sales.** Encourage customers to communicate with you and place orders through the Web. That can lower your phone bills, especially if your customers normally use your toll-free number to order your products. It will also reduce your processing, postage, and marketing expenditures.

Find out how they rate your services, what would motivate them to buy more often from you, and how to reach out to more customers like them.

The expense is well worth it. There's no quicker way and probably no better way to conduct market research.
—*The Working Communicator* newsletter

182 **Get student support.** Enlist the services of local student volunteers for your newsletter and other marketing materials. Offer bylines, credit lines, and other recognition in return for their help.

Contact the art, graphic design, marketing, or related departments at local high schools.

You'll find teachers eager to give their student "real world experience"—sometimes for nothing more than a class lecture or two by you.

183 Communicate by calendar. Publicize events in which you're involved in the calendar sections of appropriate publications. Normally the calendar editors will print the information for free.

184 Conduct your business over breakfast. It's the cheapest meal to buy, and you can hold your meeting without cutting into your normal working hours.

Breakfast meetings tend to be more productive. They're tops on everyone's daily agenda, minds are fresh, no alcohol is served, and there's a built-in deadline.

185 Broadcast your message for free. Inform TV and radio talk show producers of your expertise, and of your availability to share it on the air on short notice. The producers frequently face program changes and cancellations, and need last-minute fill-ins. (For additional TV talk show tips, see Chapter 6.)

186 Host a show. Approach a cable access channel or AM radio station about presenting a program.

Those are the broadcast outlets that are most accessible to first-time program hosts.

Provide information about the format you have in mind, program topics, guests, and reasons why the show would appeal to their viewers or listeners.

If you get the go-ahead, get the tapes. The video and audio tape copies of the programs will serve you well as personal marketing tools.

187 Use events organized by others to make contacts and seal deals. For example, a financial advisor used a business-opportunity event promoted by others to plaster windshields with his own flyer.

The good news: Seminar promoters spend big money to get people to attend their events. The better news: You can prospect with those people when they get there.

—*1001 Ways to Market Your Services* by Rick Crandall

188 Sell your stuff on the radio. A radio talk-show appearance gives you an opportunity and an audience to sell your products and yourself.

For best results, radio talk show expert Joe Sabah suggests that you:

- tell your listeners to have a pencil ready to record some "important information." Then they can jot down your phone number when you provide it later.
- ask the station for permission to advise listeners to contact the station for your number.
- thank the host and producer after the show, and offer to return.

189 **Gift certificates help you gain a lot while giving up little.**
Gain business by offering certificates and coupons. Those who redeem those certificates are unlikely to do so alone. That means new prospects, and new opportunities for you to sell.

190 **Give the gift of someone else's gift certificate.**
Approach other companies about supplying you with gift certificates or discount coupons you can use for your own marketing purposes.

Consider movie passes, dining discount cards, spa coupons, car wash certificates or similar gifts for your top customers.

Approach potential "suppliers" with the idea that you can help promote their business. By distributing their certificates, you give them more exposure and increase their sales

191 **Check into free directories.**
According to a study by the Association of Industrial Advertisers, when buyers look for sellers, 35 percent find them in business directories. Virtually every industry has one.

Check in the library under *Directories in Print*, published by Gale Research (800-877-4253).
—*Big Marketing Ideas for Small Service Businesses* by Marilyn and Tom Ross

192 **Use all your space.** Make the most of all the space allotted to you in a free directory. You lose out when you include only your name, address and phone numbers. Use the extra lines to describe your benefits and diversity of services.

193 **"No pay" publications.**
You can get free issues of any publication by contacting the publishers and indicating your interest in advertising. Request as many back issues as possible.

That will save you money when you're considering whether to promote yourself in the publication. And it's cheap way to find out if a publication ran the article or other information that you submitted to them.

194 **Ask for freebies to share.**
Request complimentary copies of directories, magazines, and other resources that you can share within your client base, association, or industry.

Publishers sometimes are willing to provide free copies if they think that doing so will get them good exposure and future business.

A public relations consultant, for example, might request a complimentary media directory from a publisher in return for the promise to promote it as a resource to her Fortune 500 customers.

195 **Join your group's membership committee.**
Whether you're active in an association, trade group, chamber of commerce, or other organization, your efforts to increase their membership will mean business for you. There's great prospecting potential in the membership appointments you conduct on behalf of your group. You'll get widespread exposure within your industry and community, and will establish important relationships as the liaison between incoming members and the group.

196 Host **"come over to my place" events.** Seminars, workshops, product demonstrations, brown bag lunch events—call them what you will, but consider them good personal marketing.

Lure people in with the promise of good information and practical tips— and then follow through on your promise. Better yet, exceed their expectations.

Give them free ideas they can use—and they may give you their business.

197 Meet at your place. Arrange to meet customers, prospects, and others at your office when possible.

Not only do you save on the time and expense of local travel, you have easy access to all of your own materials. That avoids the hassle of having to mail or ship information later.

By hosting the meeting, you can better control the agenda, flow and timing.

198 Take your office on the road. Take advantage of big events— conventions, trade shows, annual meetings—to connect face-to-face with out-of-town prospects and customers.

But don't rely on random contacts. Avoid any guesswork and missed connections by scheduling definite appointments in definite locations. Even a brief get-together may have far more impact and cost less than future phone, online, or mail contacts.

199 Take your self-promotion hat with you. Make the most of your out-of-town business trips by scheduling as many prospecting appointments as time will allow.

Let prospects know that you "will be in town anyway" and that you would be available to stop by to present your materials. Recommend that they invite (other) decision makers to the meeting.

In addition, use the trip to visit any of your clients in the area.

200 Phone from home. For home businesses, make outgoing calls on your personal line. Local calls are generally less expensive when dialed from a personal line, and it frees up your business line for incoming calls.

CHAPTER FIVE

Maximize Your Marketing Materials

Making a good first impression isn't enough.
You need to make a good *lasting* impression.

I t takes more than just enthusiasm and commitment to promote yourself successfully. It takes more than just positive first impressions. It takes materials that establish your identity and convey your professionalism, uniqueness, and expertise.

Preparation is vital to your success. If you show up at an appointment with a briefcase full of nothing more than product and service information, then you're not prepared.

Your briefcase should also contain marketing materials that spell out the benefits and advantages that *you* offer. Your personal-sale information is every bit as important as your product information.

Impressive marketing materials can help you go from merely acting the part of a successful professional to *looking* the part, as well.

Polished, professional-looking marketing materials will continue to sell you long after you've walked out the door or hung up the phone.

Skilled self-promoters will do whatever's necessary to get their foot in the door and make a powerful personal presentation. But they understand that the impression that counts is the one that remains after they walk out the door.

They understand that they need to leave a paper trail.

Your Paper Trail

The paper you leave behind may well determine if your deal gets sealed, your contract gets signed, or your proposal gets approved.

Your "paper" should do more than inform others how they can reach you. It must show them *why* they should reach you. It should convey not only what you do, but how well you do it—and how you're uniquely qualified to do it.

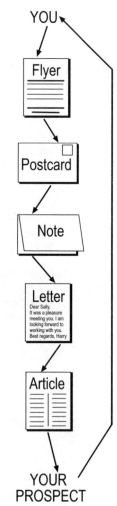

Your marketing materials play a crucial role in your personal sales efforts. They help you create and reinforce a personal impression. They help establish your professional identity, demonstrate your expertise, and sell you when you are not there to sell yourself.

Marketing materials supplement your self-promotion efforts. They showcase your credentials, your skills, and the benefits others get when they retain your services. And they describe the products and services that you offer.

Promotional materials keep you in touch and connected during the "ponder period"—the time span during which prospects decide whether to work with you. It's the time they say they need to "think it over," to weigh their options.

A Paper Campaign

The more time that passes, the less likely prospects are to act—or even think about you. You must use that time to launch a steady flow of marketing materials—a paper campaign.

Those materials can include personal notes, postcards, memos, article reprints, flyers, new product brochures—whatever it takes to keep your name in front of your prospects and the lines of communication open.

Your persistence will pay off. Studies cited in the book *Guerrilla Selling* show that it takes nine impressions to move a prospect from total apathy to purchase readiness. While only four percent of sales are made on the first call, over 80 percent are made after the eighth call.

If, ultimately, things don't work out—a deal falls through, negotiations break down, a proposal gets rejected—it may have nothing to do with what you said. But it may have everything to do with what you left behind—or didn't.

Personalizing Your Package

The marketing pieces you leave behind will vary considerably in their format and content. But you can add consistency to those pieces by including a few common elements.

One of those elements is identification and address information.

All of your marketing materials should contain all of your business addresses and all of your business phone numbers. There are no exceptions here. There's no reason why anyone should be unaware of your office and e-mail addresses, or your telephone, fax, and pager numbers.

Your promotional information must indicate how and where to reach you—all day, every day. One of your key challenges as a self-promoter is to make yourself fully accessible and available to those who seek to reach you.

Your logo is another element that should be common to all of your marketing pieces. Every marketing item—from lug-

---

Consistency Builds Your Image

There should be consistency in both the theme and the look of your marketing efforts. You need a consistent look and "feel" so that people recognize your materials at a glance. Otherwise, you communicate that you are disorganized.

Consistency in color and typeface also can help you tie your marketing materials together. Adopt at least one color, and at least one style of type to use on all of your materials.

gage tags and address labels to one-sheets and Web pages—should bear your logo (or that of your company).

Labels, by the way, provide one of the simplest ways to extend your paper trail. By now, you know better than to give anything to anyone without putting your name on it. Labels get the job done as well as anything.

Your Distinctive Style

Before recreating your personal marketing materials, have a look at those of your competitors. Review the one-sheets, bio sheets, resumes, and other forms distributed by other professionals in your field. Study the brochures, catalogs, annual reports, price lists, and other information that competing organizations send out.

The idea is to learn what services those competitors offer—and how they *present* those services in their promotional literature. Visit their Web pages. You'll find out a great deal about their services, products, prices, and clients.

An effective way to list *your* services is to include them on that most basic of marketing tools: your business card.

Chances are there's insufficient space on your card to list all your products and services. But can you include the major ones—and the major benefits buyers receive from them?

Add one thing more to your business card: your photograph.

A photograph? On your business card? But that's something people in your field just *don't* do, you say.

Never mind. Do it. Include your photo on your business card. And on your letterhead. And on your Web page. And on all the other materials that you distribute.

Nothing differentiates you, nor establishes your identity, better than your photo. Others may have the

same job title or offer similar services to the same kind of clients—but no one *looks* exactly like you do.

Prospects and others you seek to influence will forget your name. They'll forget your title and company name. They're less likely to forget your face.

Customize Your Material

People will react more favorably to you when you adapt your marketing mix to fit their needs and interests. Speak directly to their needs with personalized and customized marketing materials. You can easily adapt the promotional pieces that are in your computer—like client lists and testimonials.

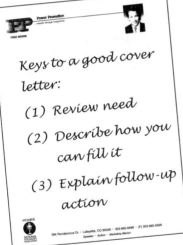

Begin by customizing your cover letter, the marketing piece that usually gets read first.

Never doubt the value of an effective cover letter—nor the problems created by an ineffective one.

Cover letters enable you to connect with persons of influence. You can build a strong connection in your letters if you begin by acknowledging their needs, then explain how you can meet them.

A good cover letter reviews a previously-stated need ("You said you're seeking an experienced attorney you can trust"), describes how you can fill that need ("I offer experienced legal assistance to dozens of professionals like you") and states a follow-up action step ("I will recontact you Thursday afternoon").

Boost Your Benefits

Your primary goal in writing a cover letter is to address the needs of the recipient. But what if you don't *know* that individual? What if the letter is part of a random direct mail campaign? Or if your letter is a response to an agency's request for proposals, requiring you to send your materials prior to the interview?

In those cases, emphasize the benefits you offer. Make it clear early in your letter that you help others make money, save money and time, work more efficiently, etc.

For too many professionals, the cover letter is little more than an afterthought. They quickly and carelessly put it together only after they assemble the rest of their marketing package. The result: misspellings, grammatical errors, and misinformation.

Those you write to may never *get* to your other marketing materials if your cover letter turns them off. If the letter fails to address their needs, or fails to explain the ways you can help them, or contains factual and other errors, then the rest of your marketing materials won't matter.

Hold the Brochures

Many marketing consultants will attempt to convince you that you must develop a brochure for yourself or your business. They will declare its great promotional

> "Brochures tell, but seldom sell."
> —Rick Crandall,
> *Marketing Your Services*

value, and point out that the more colors and graphics you can include (in other words, the more money you invest), the better.

Don't believe it. Don't use brochures. They get too dated, too fast. Too often they end up gathering dust on an office shelf, out of sight and out of mind.

It happened to me. When I launched my speaking career, I spent several hundred dollars on a very fancy, very colorful brochure on very fancy, very heavy stock. It was something to behold—and I beheld, on every chance I got.

One day I decided to change my list of speaking topics. I needed to add a topic to my list that was attracting considerable interest: "Free Publicity: How to Get Quoted and Promoted in the Media." Also, I wanted to delete a self-esteem topic which had not been well received.

Suddenly, my very flashy brochure was obsolete. The topic list was out of date, and there wasn't much I could do about it. Oh, I toyed with the idea of printing up an insert with the revised list. That would have meant more money and more confusion: one brochure with two separate sets of topics.

I pondered the possibility of including an insert describing the free publicity presentation. Then I realized that I would have to go through that effort every time I developed a new program.

I scrapped the plan and stuck the outdated brochures on a shelf, determined to soon find a way to use them. Soon never came. One rainy afternoon, I deep-sixed those personal promotion brochures.

If you are absolutely, positively, unquestionably committed to brochures, review tips 248–250 at the end of this chapter.

Promotional Kits

A better bet than a brochure is a personal promotion kit. A personal promotion kit is a folder into which you insert your most timely and relevant information. It allows you the flexibility to change your marketing message and materials at any time and keep your contacts up-to-date on what you have to offer.

A sales rep seeking to close a deal can provide her kit along with the product information. An entrepreneur seeking corporate sponsorship can provide executives with a kit containing articles demonstrating his or her industry expertise.

A home-based business owner bidding on a city government contract can enclose his kit with his proposal.

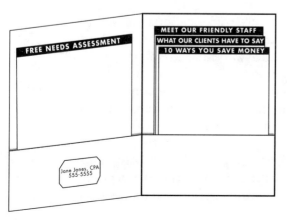

The more you customize your kit to your prospect's situation, the more impact it will have. Include a personalized cover letter along with pertinent articles by and about you, a client list, and testimonial letters. Add a list of your most appropriate services, products and skills, and references and recommendations from movers and shakers.

Round out your kit with any other material that demonstrates your expertise and qualifications. Consider work samples—sample proposals, business plans, blueprints, contracts, portfolios, or similar documents.

Finally, add a list of your distinctions to your kit. Include the top ten reasons you differ from your competitors. Add ten "only" statements—ten skills or achievements that apply only to you. Finish off with a list of the ten major benefits others receive from dealing with you.

Store components of your marketing kit on your computer, altering them as the need arises. This allows you to adjust your resume, bio sheet, and product and service lists to make them more relevant to specific prospects and clients.

> "The more customized your approach is to your audience, the better you'll do."
> —Bill Brooks,
> *Niche Selling*

Your Media Kit

It's easy to convert your personal promotion kit into a media kit. You can make it available as a resource for the reporters, editors, producers, and others who cover your industry.

You'll read more in the next chapter about establishing relationships with the media. But it's worth noting here that your kit will catch the attention of editors if it contains information that will help them do their jobs.

You might include a list of questions frequently asked about your industry—and your answers to them. Throw in a list of story ideas, and names of other valuable sources of information.

A quality photograph is an essential component of a marketing/media kit. Invest in a good promotional photograph; anything less just won't do. Select a photographer who can provide you with a flattering set of prints, including a large number of 5″ × 7″, black-and-white glossies. Also useful for promotional purposes: some color reproductions and "action" shots showing you on the job.

Once you assemble an impressive personal portfolio, you'll be tempted to send out the entire package immediately to movers and shakers everywhere—and even to new prospects.

Bad idea!

Sending too much too soon is a temptation to which many self-promoters unwisely succumb. Just as a fisherman shouldn't grab for his largest net before he has the fish on the line, you don't want to grab for your entire set of marketing materials to send to new prospects.

Give 'em *all* that you've got at an early stage and you risk overwhelming them. There's the very real danger that your package, delivered by mail or courier, will end up in the "Get To Later" file. The problem is, if the package is too big, recipients may never get to it at all.

Then, there's the financial consideration. It costs money to mail or ship your materials—big money. It's not the kind of money you should invest until you perceive legitimate interest. Even then, you should dispatch your materials in stages, whetting, but never spoiling, the appetite on the other end.

The One-Sheet

A one-sheet is among the most effective self-marketing tools. This two-sided personal promotion piece summarizes your qualifications, capabilities, services, and experience, and includes your photo and some testimonial endorsements. It should be printed on high-quality paper. The one-sheet doesn't tell your whole story, but it tells as much as prospects need to know.

You have a few things going for you by sending out a one-sheet well before shipping a large promotional packet. For one thing, you save money. For another, you increase the chances your stuff will get read.

Let's face it. People—even high-powered, influential people with fancy titles and fancy salaries to match—are lazy. And, justified or not, they're convinced they're busy. They're much more likely to review a capsulized account than a complete one.

A less impressive and less expensive alternative or supplement to a one-sheet, the two-sided promotional flyer can be printed on less expensive paper or duplicated on a copy machine.

As to what to put on that flyer, anything goes. Reprint an article by or about you on one side, and a list of your products and services on the other. Reproduce a general interest article on one side, and a list of the benefits you offer on the other. Or, put a testimonial letter on one side, a bio sheet on the other.

That two-sided flyer presents plenty of possibilities. It gives you a double dose of exposure for a minimal investment.

Personal Notes

Flyers fall into the broad category of "stay-in-touch" materials. Add personal notes to that category—handwritten notes expressing appreciation, congratulations, friendship, sympathy, or other sentiments.

It's too bad personal note-writing is fast becoming a lost art. Well-written notes can go a long way toward warming up the coldest of prospects. They help you build relationships with those prospects, so that they will think of you as more than just a "vendor."

Customize standard marketing pieces by adding personal notes to them. A note transforms

9 Reasons to Write Personal Notes

- to follow up on a meeting
- to follow up on a telephone contact
- to follow up on a referral
- to apologize
- to say "thank you"
- to welcome new customers
- to give congratulations
- to say that you saw them in the news
- to announce when you'll call

John--
  The Chamber of Commerce mixer was super. I appreciate your inviting me.

your promotional material from impersonal information that a secretary may send to something personal that *you* send.

Postcards

Postcards are a great way to send quick, unique personal notes. They're easy to write, easy to create on your computer (via a variety of postcard software programs), and easy to typeset, mail, read, and keep.

Postcards are so easy to write, in fact, that many professionals bring along a bunch on their business travels, write them on the plane on their way home from a big meeting, and mail them at the airport. It's a timely way to express appreciation, or pass along other personal greetings to movers and shakers.

Put pizzazz in your personal promotion postcards by including an imprinted marketing message, your logo, your photo, and space for a personal note and address.

The format and size of these cards can vary. You'll see cards with the photo, imprinted marketing message and logo on one side, and the note and address space on the flip side.

Then there are the cards where the marketing information is combined with the personal note space on one side, and the photo, logo and address on the other.

Any size postcard will be effective, but remember that cards 4" x 6" or smaller go at the postcard rate, while larger cards require first-class letter postage.

The common denominator is that all of these cards enable you to transmit your personal sentiments as well as your professional message in a way that's painless for you to send, and for others to read.

Newsletters

Newsletters can serve your personal promotion needs in many ways. Use them to update others on your achievements and awards, your new products or services, your clients, and the recognition that you've received.

Use them to share your successes, your news and your views with those you seek to influence, those you serve, those you would like to serve, and those you used to and would like to again serve.

Certain elements belong in your newsletter, whether you generate it on your own computer, or rely on an outside

> ## Use Your Newsletter to Promote Yourself with the Press
>
> Tom Peters suggests you consider the media as a customer for your newsletter and other marketing materials.
>
> "In today's environment with more competition, more products and more media, the press can be an ally," he points out.
>
>

printer to do the job. Your newsletter should contain self-promotional information, newsworthy material, articles by and about your prospects and clients, and perhaps a survey or two.

The timely and topical information in your newsletter will appeal to the media and will help you generate free publicity.

Increase interest in and demand for your newsletter by featuring stories about those who use your services. Run their photos and other promotional information with those stories, and they'll circulate copies of "their" issues.

Talk up your prospects and clients in your newsletter, and they'll talk *you* up. Demand for your newsletter will grow as others seek coverage in it.

Another advantage of newsletters is that they can serve as market research tools. Learn the future needs of those you seek to reach, and simultaneously elicit referrals and testimonial comments from them by including a questionnaire in your newsletter.

Newsletters: Time Well Spent

Do periodic newsletters—or personal promotion letters—require a lot of time to prepare and distribute? You betcha. But self-promoters who regularly pursue this strategy consider it time well-spent.

Cliff Albert considered it a good investment of his time. I met Albert, the news director of San Diego's KFMB Radio, at a convention of the Radio-TV News Directors Association. It was during my stint running my broadcast news service in Washington in the mid-1980s, an era when an increasing number of radio stations were cutting their news budgets in favor of less costly music programming.

But Albert's news department flourished, and station management didn't hesitate to approve his budget requests. One reason: Albert's "News from Dr. News" newsletter. Albert used that publication to keep the managers informed of all the stories his news team broke, all the positive feedback his department received, and all the ways KFMB News generated income for the station.

Two-Way Communication

Danielle Kennedy, author of seven sales books and audio and video sales training programs, stresses the "need to spend more time communicating to our customers about what we are doing for them."

We also need to get feedback from our customers as to whether we're living up to our promises—and their expectations.

Evaluation forms supply us with that feedback. You can use the forms to measure your performance, and to market your services. A good way to remind customers that you're there is to ask their opinion of how you're doing.

Marketing questions to include on your feedback forms:

- What did you find to be the most valuable part of the service I provided?
- When is the next time you may need the services of a _____? *(fill in the blank with your profession)*
- Who else do you know who might be interested in my services?

Answers to these questions will supply you with testimonials, leads for follow-up business, and referrals, respectively. Feedback forms aren't just good business; they're good marketing.

Your Marketing Materials Help Make You

Effective marketing materials help you become—and come across as—a successful professional.

Establish your own identify on all the promotional pieces you distribute. That means sharing your own logo, photo, and commercial message.

If that creates friction within the organization you work for, maintain two sets of promotional materials, the company's and your own. Include something of yourself even when you're sending out the company's information.

Your personal marketing materials should "play you up"—and downplay your principal employer. If you're employed by a company, mention it in your personal promotional materials the way the company would include a major client in their materials. In other words, list it—and leave it at that.

Remember that no matter who your principal employer is, customers must "buy" you before they'll buy what you sell. Your materials should help them make both of those purchases.

Your Own "Baseball Cards"

You can get quite creative in your self-promotion. Police in many communities, for example, distribute trading cards to boost their image among local children.

The cards, which feature a glossy photo of the officer on the front and some personal information (like years on the force and hobbies) on the back, are targeted at elementary school children. Often they contain a message, such as "Help us stop crime." *The Wall Street Journal* reports that the "cop cards" help by "humanizing the officers and portraying them in the heroic light of star athletes." The idea is to help the officers counteract and "fight the appeal of rich, slick drug dealers."

Officer Lena Poole

Action Ideas and Tips

201 **Make your letterhead sell you.** Don't just use your organization's name, address and numbers on your letterhead. Include the same information about yourself, along with your photograph. List the groups to which you belong and your title(s).

Add a list of major awards you've won or degrees you've received. Other possibilities: your "only" commercial and a benefit statement ("I help companies increase their profits by ....").

202 **Make your logo sell you.** What's the one image you want others to associate with you or your company? That's the image your logo should reflect.

Do you want others to think of you as strong? Wise? Caring? Dependable? Dedicated? Lean and mean?

Approach graphic designers with that image in mind. Have them create the best possible pictorial representation of it.

203 **Customize your cover letter.** Show how you can help others increase their profits or achieve their other goals. Demonstrate in the letter your knowledge of their organization and industry, and show how your expertise makes you the most qualified to fulfill their needs.

204 **Create a "killer" card.** "Get the best business card money can buy. Engrave it, foil stamp it, logo it, graphic design it, multicolor it. The acid test: if you give out your card and the recipient doesn't say, 'Nice card,' get it redone."
—Jeffrey Gitomer, in *Entrepreneur* magazine

205 **Dare to be different.** Put your photo on your business card. Set the card in a vertical, rather than horizontal format. Use both sides: one for contact information, the other for a list of your products and services. Include a special customer offer. ("Present this card for a 10% discount on your first purchase.")

Include any and all of your numbers: business and home phone, digital pager, fax, e-mail, Web page addresses, etc.

206 **Add a slogan.** Examples: "On-Site Fax Repair," "24-Hour Emergency Repair Service," "Catering With Finesse," "Same-Day Service," "Calls Answered Around the Clock," "In business since 1979."
—*Getting Business to Come to You* by Paul & Sarah Edwards and Laura Clampitt Douglas

207 **Stick to it.** Have a printer reproduce your card on labels. Stick them on gifts, notes, books, manuals, and any other items that you distribute.

Labels have the sticking power that standard cards do not. Affix your business card labels to everything, and you'll make a lasting impact.

|208| **Develop a business card "brag book."** Have your customers jot down on the backs of their cards two or three reasons why they chose to do business with you. Or ask them to write down the two best aspects of your service.

Put the cards in clear plastic sleeves, and insert them in a binder.

|209| **Assess the alternatives.** Examples of alternatives to standard business cards:
* printed Rolodex™ cards
* double-sized cards folded in half (they can work as mini-brochures, with standard information on front, and additional benefits and details inside)
* laminated cards containing your tips or other words of wisdom along with your phone numbers and address

|210| **Picture this.** Enclose photos when submitting an article, or when providing personal information to a publication. Include "action" photos along with your standard head shots. Supply suggested "cutlines" (captions) in the event the publication chooses to run your photo but not the accompanying story.

|211| **Be seen before you're heard.** Include a photo with the information you send to groups that invite you to speak. Suggest that they use it for promotional purposes, and request copies of the promotional pieces they distribute.

|212| **Get the picture.** Add a digital camera to your arsenal of personal promotion weapons. Use it to transmit your likeness online, insert new and improved photos in your Web page and other business communications, and create marketing tools like calendars and cards.

|213| **Focus on others.** Have your picture taken with an individual you seek to impress. Enlarge the photo, and send it to him or her with a nice note.

Or, snap a photo of your customer receiving delivery of your products, or signing the contract for your services. Send it along with a thank-you or congratulatory note.

|214| **Create a personal promotion kit.** Include:
* a promotional "one-sheet"
* a personal bio sheet
* reprints of articles by and about you
* testimonial letters and comments
* a products and services list
* promotional photograph(s)
* a client list
* a reference list
* work samples

|215| **Fit your kit to your page.** Adapt your personal promotion kit so that you can add it to your

Web page, and develop a version that you can send out by fax.

Use a heavy, laminated portfolio or folder with a business card holder and pockets for the "paper" version of your kit. The contents should be of the highest quality; use cover stock paper and color reprints, when possible. Aim for consistency in the font sizes and colors used in the promotional pieces.

216 **Flip it.** Use the flip side of article reprints for personal memos and a list of clients, products, services, references, recent achievements, etc.

217 **Play the numbers.** Use numbers ("$50 off") instead of percentages ("Save 35 percent") to express savings, when using ads, mailers, or other promotional pieces. Direct mail experts say that percentages involve the kind of "translation" that most people find difficult, and that 50 percent is the only one that people fully understand.

Even so, "half off" means more to most people than "50 percent off," and phrases like "Buy one, get one free" have even more impact.

218 **Reprint your best ads.** Use them as circulars, handouts, and direct mail pieces, and add them to your personal promotion kit. Enlarge your best ads to poster size, mount them, and use them as signs at your office.

219 **Upgrade and update.** Keep your materials fresh by updat-

ing personal photos and lists of clients, services and references. Replace dated article reprints and testimonial letters, eliminate other dated information, and improve the packaging of your materials.

220 **Delete dates.** Extend the "shelf life" of article reprints, testimonial letters, and other materials by using correction fluid to delete their dates before you photocopy them. Discard those materials that appear dated even after the date has been removed from them.

221 **Get connected.** Insert words and phrases in your marketing materials that directly relate to the recipients of those materials. If you're a software salesman approaching an engineering firm, for example, refer in your product list to software products *available to engineers.* If you're a consultant trying to impress an accounting firm, revise your bio sheet to indicate that you help *accountants and others* increase their profits.

222 **Add the personal touch to your fax cover sheet.** Include your photo on the sheet, and a promotional tagline that identifies—and differentiates—you. Provide your sales reps, office staff and others within your organization with their own personalized fax cover sheets.

The personalized sheets send the message that you take pride in your services and yourselves.

223 **Send facts by fax.** Provide faxable promotional material like testimonial letters, your bio or article reprints during or *immediately after* your telephone conversation with a prospect. Materials transmitted by fax or e-mail supplement any favorable impression you make over the phone. But that impression diminishes if you allow too much time to pass.

224 **One-derful sheets.** Summarize important information about yourself and your company on a single, two-sided sheet. Your "one-sheet" should include a few paragraphs of biographical information, your photo, a list of your products and services, a client list, and testimonial comments from clients or references.

225 **Customize your one-sheet.** Insert industry-specific information or create different versions for different target audiences. Well-written one-sheets add value to your service by explaining the value of getting *you* along with the service.

Include at least one extra color, a variety of font sizes and other imaginative graphic design offset by ample white space.

Adapt your one-sheet for use on your Web page and for transmission over your fax machine.

226 **Reach for your resume.** A resume can "reduce anxiety and build trust." A resume that elaborates on your most significant positions, and the results you achieved, is more effective than one that provides little

more than a shopping list of all your past jobs.

—Let Your Customers Do the Talking
by Michael E. Cafferky

227 **Postcards should contain a call to action** ("Register now to qualify for the sale price") or a preview of *your* next action ("I'll e-mail you with contract details").

228 **Multiple mailings.** Follow a direct mail piece with at least two additional mailings within 45 days, says marketing guru Dan Kennedy. If it can work for collection agencies, he reasons, it can work for you.

Other experts advise sending up to four mailings spaced a week apart, and following up with a phone call within five days of your final mailing.

229 **Include a "P.S."** Studies show that 80 percent of all recipients read that part of the letter.

230 **Make your direct mail look like personal mail.** Address the envelopes by hand, rather than using computerized mailing labels. Hand stamp the envelopes, rather than running them through a postal meter. Include *your* name and return address on the envelopes, but not your company name and logo. Avoid using a post office box number.

231 **Make it easier to buy.**

• Offer a credit card payment option (it will increase your orders by 15%)

- Offer a toll-free number (it will triple your response rate)
- Offer a "bill me" option

232 **Direct mail dos.**
- Create a sense of urgency ("This offer expires May 6.").
- Include an "active" close ("I'll call you Tuesday") rather than a "passive" one ("I look forward to hearing from you.").
- Follow with a phone call within 72 hours after your mailing is received (it can increase your response rate by 18 percent) .

233 **Make it brief and believable.** Write a marketing letter that gets results by including:
- an attention-grabbing headline that offers an important benefit
- unique features and benefits of your service
- one central and simple idea
- believable testimonials
- a guarantee
- an organized, easy-to-read format
- a clear call for action
- a P.S.

—*Big Marketing Ideas for Small Service Businesses* by Marilyn and Tom Ross

234 **Include "winning" words in your direct mail.** Use words such as:

- action
- benefit
- can
- discover
- easy
- free
- guaranteed
- health
- introducing
- join
- know
- love
- money
- magic
- new
- opportunity
- proven
- quality
- results
- save
- today
- urgent
- win
- you

235 **Make it lumpy.** Include an audio- or videocassette, a product sample or even a piece of candy. Use mailing materials that differ in color, texture, and shape from other envelopes and packages.

236 **If you're planning a direct marketing campaign, plan on January, February, September, or October.**
These are the best months for direct marketing because they signify the beginning of the new year, the coming of spring, the school year, and the winter season, respectively. The worst months: July and August, because people are so involved with outdoor activities and vacations.

237 **The worse the weather, the better the climate for direct marketing.** (The exception is December when many people are distracted by holiday activities and travel.)
Also, plan for your mail to arrive on Tuesday, Wednesday or Thursday,

but avoid sending it so it arrives the first week of the month.
—*Guerrilla Marketing Attack* by Jay Conrad Levinson

238 Put out the flyer. Flyers are among the most versatile self-promotional tools. Use them for hand-outs, inserts in newspapers or company newsletters, and direct mail. Try them at trade shows and other events, and on bulletin boards, networking tables at business gatherings, etc.

Use eye-catching graphics and colors, and keep your message simple.

239 Follow the AIDA formula. AIDA stands for: grab **A**ttention, create **I**nterest, develop **D**esire, gener-ate **A**ction.

Use a headline stating the key ben-efit ("Home Owners: Save Money by Refinancing Now"), and introduce other benefits with phrases like "You'll learn...," "You'll receive....," "You'll save..." Include a call to action ("Call for a free sample") and use "you" regularly.
—*Win-Win Marketing* (report on flyers), San Jose, CA

240 Scout it out. Determine the public facilities (office buildings, malls, libraries, etc.) where it would be best to promote your services. Contact the management at those facilities and ask that they post your flyers and other materials on bulletin boards and other locations.

241 Create a newsletter. Use it to promote yourself, share news about your products and services, dis-play your appreciation for your clients, and elicit information on buying habits.

While self promotion is your key goal, it has to be subtle. Newsletters that are blatantly self-serving get ig-nored. Focus your newsletter on giving—advice, support, information, news. That way you'll *get* a lot in return—business, customer loyalty, visibility, respect, and a whole lot more.

242 Make it a keeper. Features like these will influence readers to *keep* your newsletters:
- tips
- summaries of business ideas from other sources
- warnings of dangers, scams or other bad news related to your industry
- calendars of events (like trade shows and business expos) and deadlines
- "how to" articles
- details on free or extra services that you offer
- client buy/sell "swap shop" info
- area sports and entertainment schedules

243 Encourage them to keep it. Three-hole punch your news-letters. This reinforces the notion that your newsletter is worthy of saving. Even better—send readers a binder in which to store your newsletters. You can have binders printed with the name of your newsletter. Or use binders with clear plastic overlays under which you can insert a page imprinted with the name of your newsletter, the name of your company, and contact information.

244 **Send your newsletter to the media.** Include at least one "hard news" story in each issue. Promote the story to reporters via releases and e-mail messages. One story possibility: the results of a poll of your clients on a key issue in the news.

Include occasional articles based on interviews with trade press reporters in your field. That might influence those reporters to refer to or reprint the article in which they've been featured.

245 **"Comp" your clients.** Offer copies of your newsletter to clients so that they can distribute them to *their* clients. It will make your clients look good, and get your name out to more people.

Send additional copies to professionals in allied fields, and local civic and business organizations.

246 **You show mine, I'll show yours.** Develop cooperative distribution arrangements for your newsletter and other promotional materials. Ask clients and friends to display your newsletter in their offices, and to include your materials in the information they send to contacts. Offer to do the same for them.

247 **Set up reciprocal newsletter relationships.** Offer to run articles in your newsletter by or about influential companies and individuals in your field in return for the same kind of exposure in *their* newsletters.

248 **The simpler the language, the better the brochure.**
Avoid jargon, formal words or stilted language. Focus on the benefits of your services, rather than on their features, and use "bullets" to list them. Avoid using dates (they can make your brochure out-of-date) and too much data.

249 **Pages, not panels.** Design your brochure to follow a page, rather than panel-by-panel format. Don't restrict your headline and graphics with panel boundaries. Have the graphics flow across the whole page. That way you can use larger type and illustrations, and make a greater impact.

250 **Consider the "shelf life."** In deciding how many copies of your brochure to print, consider, for example, whether yours is a seasonal brochure (good for three months), or whether it's an overview piece that may hold up for about two years.

Determine your quantities accordingly, and then increase your estimates by 15 percent to account for unexpected uses.

—Dave Voracek, aka the "Brochure Doctor"

CHAPTER SIX

Write It Down and Speak Up

"Say it loud and say it proud—in print and from the platform."
—Fred Berns

Get the word out to as many people as possible, as quickly as possible.

That's your game plan if you're serious about making the personal sale. The best way to carry out that plan is through "smart marketing," the fine art of making a maximum impact for a minimal investment of time and money.

In order to rise above the competition, you must get your message out to as many prospects as possible, as rapidly and economically as possible. Go beyond the cold calls and word-of-mouth referrals on which your competitors depend. Instead, rely on such "think big" strategies as free publicity and public speaking.

The Best Advertising That Money *Can't* Buy

Free publicity is any positive information about you or your organization that appears in print, on the air, or, in some cases, online.

Publicity is that two-sentence blurb about you in an online or in-house newsletter about your promotion. It's that feature in a business journal about your company's expansion plans. It's your letter to the editor in a local news-

YOUR LOCAL PAPER

In the news...
Karen Jhin Wins
Regional Award
Local insurance
agent Karen Jhin
was commended
for providing out-
standing customer
service by the
State Association

paper about regional hiring practices.

It's your article on industry trends in a trade association magazine. It's your guest appearance on a local radio talk show. It's the 30-second feature about your award on the local TV news.

Unfortunately, few executives, entrepreneurs, or employees give much thought to the idea of writing, or getting written about. They are much more familiar with the practice of paying to promote their services—in print (as in Yellow Pages ads), on the air (radio and TV spots), or online (Web page advertising). Some may even agree with Jerry Della Femina, the innovative advertising executive who once observed that "advertising is the most fun you can have with your clothes on." Expensive fun, but fun nevertheless.

Department store magnate John Wanamaker, for one, wasn't so sure. "I know half of my advertising is a waste of money," he said. "But I don't know which half."

Free publicity offers the kind of credibility that advertising does not. In virtually all cases, an article or broadcast news report about you will have far greater impact than an ad.

Here, There, and Everywhere

Free publicity is anywhere and everywhere, and it comes in many flavors.

You need only look in the local newspaper's business pages or the area business journal to see free publicity at work. All those "names in the news," all that information about promotions and awards and new contracts are examples of publicity that didn't cost anything to the person or company in the news.

Positive publicity is surprisingly easy to come by once you take the initiative. Your initiative will make the difference between getting media exposure and merely getting jealous about your competitor who is "lucky" enough to receive so much good "press."

Getting Free Publicity: Tricks of the Trade

Study print and broadcast journalism and you'll learn a thing or two about free publicity—namely, who gets it and how. Here are some rules of the road to pave the way to getting free publicity.

Easy does it. Don't get scared off because you lack journalism or public relations training. Spare yourself the expense of hiring someone to pursue press coverage for you. This really is only a two-step process: the story pitch, and the follow-up press release. No sweat.

They need you. Forget the idea that reporters and editors do *you* a favor by running your story. In fact, their jobs rely on their ability to gather information to fill space or air time every day, or week, or month. They badly need what you can give them. News.

They are busy. Don't expect the reporters you contact with your story idea to engage in casual conversation. They won't give you much time to pitch your story, and may seem downright rude. That's OK. It forces you to communicate succinctly—a good lesson to learn, anyway—and the potential outcome—positive media coverage—makes it all worthwhile.

Do their job. Reporters are not inclined to spend much time doing research for your story. Do it for them. Your chances of making a favorable impression will increase substantially if you

---

Show Your Appreciation

"When you get a good story, send a thank-you note to the reporter and the reporter's editor. This happens so seldom that reporters won't forget."

—*Take the Mystery Out of Media* by Lorraine Kingdon

provide ample background information (facts and fig-ures). Provide them with other references and informa-tion sources on the topic.

You need not be a Pulitzer Prize winner. You've been called a lot of things in your day, but a great writer isn't one of them. Not to worry. Reporters and editors are more interested in your information than in how skillfully you relay it in your press release or article. Just give them the story in your own words. They'll take it from there.

The timelier, the better. Your story's timeliness may determine if it ends up in print, on the air—or in the waste-basket. Stories for use "anytime" rarely see the light of day. Convince 'em what ya got is hot, and relate it to today's news.

The more topical, the bet-ter. So, what's in the news these days? What's the hot conversation topic? "Piggyback" your story idea onto the topic of the day or week or month and journalists are more likely to care about what you have to say.

The more focused, the bet-ter. Every media outlet seeks to relate information to its audience. Help them out. Cus-tomize your story idea so that it pertains to the read-ers/viewers/listeners.

Contact: Robin Jacobs
Vice President, Sales and Marketing
Dorwest Corp.
100 River Road
Denver, CO 80231
PHONE: 800-555-7151 FAX: 303-555-0081
E-mail:Rjacobs@dorwest.com

FOR IMMEDIATE RELEASE

Dorwest Corp. Promotes Jean Gonzales to Director of Year 2000 Operations

Dorwest Corp., a leading provider of technical outsourcing solutions, has pro-moted Jean Gonzales to director of National Year 2000 Operations. This appointment coincides with the shrinking window of opportunity for organizations to rectify

Practice makes perfect. Where have you heard *that* before? It's a prevailing truth about free publicity. As challenging as those early releases are, and as awk-ward as those first pitches seem, they'll get easier and you'll get better. I promise.

You win even when you lose. You invest all that time in promoting your story to a reporter, and he or she chooses not to run it. A wasted effort? Not at all. Through your effort, you establish or reinforce a con-tact with a reporter. That, alone, is a valuable exercise—

one which increases the likelihood that the reporter will remember you the next time.

Getting Quoted and Promoted in the Media

Free publicity is less likely to result from luck than from a calculated promotion strategy. Favorable coverage comes about when you do what's necessary to get in print and on the air.

What's necessary isn't very much. You need only contact the reporters, editors, or producers at media outlets who cover your field and send them releases summarizing your news.

The initial media contact normally requires a telephone pitch. You must, within about 15 seconds, convince reporters that you and your story idea are worthy of their attention. Don't attempt to deliver *all* the information about yourself and your idea during the brief phone conversation. Share just enough to whet their appetites for more.

The "more" that you send later (via regular mail, fax, or e-mail) is the news release, produced on your letterhead with contact information at the top, a headline, and one or two pages of copy. Include the basic who-what-where-when-why-how information in the opening paragraph.

Include at least one quote, preferably in the third or fourth paragraph. Most likely, you will quote yourself, an awkward, but interesting, exercise.

Include the most important information at the top of your release. In the (outstanding) event reporters decide to use your press release word-for-word, they probably will cut from the bottom up to accommodate space limitations.

Pay careful attention to your press release; studies indicate that the media do. The *Columbia Journalism Review* reported that 45 percent of the 188 news items in one issue of *The Wall Street Journal* came from press releases.

Articles based on your press releases *will* publicize and promote you. But before that can happen, you need to help your news come out.

The Newsmaker in You

Appreciate your own newsworthiness! Every time you sign a contract, launch a product or service, hire an employee, land a new job, win an award or promotion, create or redesign a Web page, attend a major conference, celebrate an anniversary in business, or reach any other professional milestone—that's news.

That's the kind of news the media will carry—and their readers will read. Savvy self-promoters submit more than a news release when they share their information. They also enclose a photo, thereby increasing the chances they will get even more exposure.

So what, you may ask? What's the big deal about a short blurb and your photo in a publication?

The big deal is the visibility that blurb provides. And the credibility. Get your name and photo in the newspaper, and you gain new respect. Some readers view publicity as an "endorsement" by the media of your value.

In addition, free publicity affords you a competitive edge. It's a strategic advantage to be able to identify yourself as the *only* one in your area who has been featured in a certain publication, or on a certain station.

High-Profile Publicity

Perhaps you want to go beyond the "show-and-tell" publicity drill. You seek something more than a media mention, something far bigger than a blurb.

Can do. Use the same two-step (story pitch and press release) process to elicit extensive coverage about yourself. Want a publication to interview you

Keep Your Publicity Working

Still another benefit of printed publicity is the opportunity it provides you to make reprints. Including reproductions of articles by and about you will add power to your personal portfolio. And it will establish or enhance your image as an expert.

about what's hot and what's not in your field? Want a reporter to recount your rags-to-riches success story, or recap your rapid climb up the corporate ladder, or chronicle your life in the fast lane?

You can get that kind of media attention—not as easily and not as often as the show-and-tell recognition—but you can get it.

It takes a brilliant pitch and some powerful persuasion to convince a print or broadcast outlet to develop an extensive news story or feature about you. And it takes not only an effective press release, but impressive personal marketing materials to go along with it.

None of which should be that great a challenge for a dedicated personal marketer like you. By acquiring this book, you have already demonstrated your commitment to the personal sale.

> "Self-confidence is the first requisite to great undertakings."
> —Samuel Johnson

Step one is to do some simple market research to find out the medium of choice of your target audience. Even an in-depth article by or about you in a major publication won't do you much good if the people you seek to influence don't read that publication. It's all well and good to get *The Wall Street Journal*, the *New York Times*, and *Time* magazine to run a story on you. But if your prospects are more attuned to and influenced by a regional trade publication or an online industry newsletter, your time might be better spent lining up coverage in those media.

We've focused so far on convincing the media—from in-house company newsletters to major metropolitan daily newspapers—to run a story *about* you. The alternative is to persuade them to run a story *by* you. To get publicity the first way, you often help them write the story. When you write the article under your name, you showcase your status as an "expert."

The Write Stuff

Writing an article yourself has its advantages. It gives you far more control over the content and direction of the story, and enables you to accomplish your own promotional objectives.

Think of all the topics you can cover! You can call attention to a problem ("Companies waste time and money investing in unnecessary telephone systems") and offer solutions ("They can save money and increase productivity by hiring independent telephone technology consultants, like us").

When you write the article, you can discuss trends ("More and more corporate executives now do the business travel they once delegated to middle managers"). You can offer opinions ("Mutual fund company sales charges are too high"), predictions ("The Internet will take over virtually all of the functions of business school libraries"), and analysis and commentary ("Too many organizations lose out on sales opportunities by failing to consider global expansion").

There's no guarantee that a publication will run what you write. That's why you should "prequalify" and communicate with the editors as much as possible before the fact. Share your story idea and focus, and elicit feedback before you sit down at your computer.

If you can't get a firm commitment, try to reach an understanding with the editors that they will publish your story if it meets their guidelines.

Sometimes you will get paid for your efforts; more often than not, you won't. Experienced writers know the real payoff comes in the promotional paragraph that follows the story. This "about the author" section is a golden opportunity to tout your products, your services, and yourself.

Insist that you, rather than the editor, write this promotional blurb—and milk it for what you can. Use it to share your personal commercial, list your services,

---

Headlines from Hell

For all of its advantages, free publicity has one potential disadvantage. You rarely have control over the headline attached to your story. Too often headlines convey double-meaning messages. Some recent examples:

"Safety Experts Say School Bus Passengers Should Be Belted"

"Drunk Gets Nine Months in Violin Case"

"Two Sisters Reunited after 18 Years in Checkout Counter"

"Stud Tires Out"

"Farmer Bill Dies in House"

"Red Tape Holds Up New Bridge"

"Eye Drops Off Shelf"

"Prostitutes Appeal to Pope"

"Teacher Strikes Idle Kids"

"Juvenile Court to Try Shooting Defendant"

Send a Disk

Many authors now provide editors several articles on a disk. Or, they put them online. Editors may use the articles as resources, and are more likely to run something they have on hand and computer-ready when a deadline looms.

and supply details about how others can contact you. Seek permission to include your photograph along with the write-up.

The Gift that Keeps on Giving

Whether a reporter writes your story or you do, you'll discover the power of publicity once it shows up in print. Free publicity offers long-term benefits, since a story by or about you creates a lasting impression.

A technical article in a trade journal helped launch the career of Steve Jobs, the computer whiz kid of the 1980s. The article, according to Robert Hartley in his book *Marketing Successes,* gave "considerable visibility" to Jobs and his partner, Steven Wozniak, and set Jobs on the road to owning 7.5 million Apple Computer shares worth $225 million.

Douglas Stewart reaped the profits for months after distributing a media release about his Denver company, Bird Control Inc., to the *Rocky Mountain News.* Stewart, applying a lesson he learned at my marketing program for the Colorado Pest Control Association, said that the subsequent article, on the influx of pigeons in Denver, "had the phone ringing off the hook" with thousands of dollars of new business.

Debbie Hobar, the owner of a design service for infants' rooms, derived long-lasting benefits from her four-minute appearance on a local TV "home show" in Washington, DC. Immediately after her interview on "Broadcast House Live," she received 120 calls, 25 of which turned into orders for more than $6000 in products and services.

Hobar, invited to appear on the show by a producer she called on a whim, subsequently generated even more business from her televised appearance. In the process, she raised her fees 90 percent.

When Bad Publicity Happens

The down side of free publicity is *bad* press. That's the negative information that surfaces in the media and, at least temporarily, casts shadows over you or your organization.

But rarely does bad publicity do any long-term damage. The same is true about the mistakes some reporters are sure to make, like misspelling your name, or fouling up quotes.

Self-promoters don't succumb to the challenges posed by negative publicity.

Some, in fact, welcome those challenges. They're the ones who prefer some exposure—any exposure—to no exposure at all. They're the ones who embrace the philosphy of athlete and showman Dennis Rodman that "the only bad press is an obituary."

Speaking

Write an article, and you get more than just an opportunity to appear in print. Chances are, you get a speaking topic, as well. In many cases, a topic you write about is a topic you can speak about.

Speaking before the right groups is the second of the smart marketing, one-to-many, self-promotion strategies.

Public speaking offers many of the same fringe benefits provided by free publicity. It gives you a competitive edge, since it's unlikely many of your competitors are on the speaking circuit. It's a source of visibility, since the circuit is such an effective way to get your name out and about.

Then there's credibility. Unless you say or do something to disprove it, audience members will assume that, because you're the speaker, you're the expert.

Whatever your level of speaking experience, there are plenty of speaking opportunities available to you.

> "If I went back to college again, I'd concentrate on two areas: learning to write and learning to speak before an audience. Nothing in life is more important than the ability to communicate effectively."
> —Gerald D. Ford

Consider all the groups that use outside speakers. There are trade groups within your field; service and civic groups within your community; business and professional organizations within your state. Contact your trade association for more information about speaking opportunities within your industry, and the local chamber of commerce or board of trade for a list of area groups that use outside speakers.

If you work for a large company, you may find numerous opportunities to speak within, or on behalf of, the organization.

The power of public speaking is that your influence extends well beyond those assembled in the room to hear you speak. Impress them, and they will share your information with business associates, friends, and family. Your message ultimately may reach many times the number in your original audience.

The Fear Factor

You won't find public speaking at the top of the list of America's favorite pastimes. In fact, speaking ranks high on the list of activities most people fear. Most people would prefer to do just about anything than stand up and speak in front of a group.

Then again, most people aren't self-promoters. Most people don't realize the personal promotion potential of sharing their expertise with an assembly of those with whom they would like to do business.

There are several ways to remove the "pain" from presentations—and add pizzazz. One way is to practice and get feedback on your presentations by joining Toastmasters or a similar group in your area.

Toastmasters International is the organization of nearly 8,000 clubs worldwide dedicated to helping their members improve their speaking and communication

> **Scared to Death of Speaking**
>
> "According to most studies, people's number one fear is public speaking. Number two is death. Death is number two. Does that seem right? That means to the average person, if you have to go to a funeral, you're better off in the casket than doing the eulogy."
>
> —Jerry Seinfeld, in *SeinLanguage*

skills. Consult your local directory for the clubs nearest you.

Polishing Your Presentations

It's too bad that most professionals spend virtually all of their preparation time crafting their words, and virtually none rehearsing how to present them. Polish your platform skills by focusing less on what you say, and more on how you say it.

Hiring a speech coach to help you master body language and other nonverbal skills might be a good investment, if you intend to pursue speaking as a career.

You create a new dimension for your presentations when you add visuals. In their book *TechnoSelling*, Ed Callaghan and Peter Nauert estimate that the retention factor for remembering new information 24 hours after exposure is 20 percent of what one hears; 30 percent of what one sees; and a whopping 65 percent of what one both sees *and* hears.

Who and What?

Public speaking has outstanding potential as a marketing tactic. I say "potential" because it works best if, and only if, you lay the proper groundwork ahead of time.

As with free publicity, targeting is vital. You must promote yourself to groups whose members you most want to influence. How better to make the best impression on those groups and those members than by speaking on topics that most interest them?

Generally, "pocketbook" topics make a hit. Your presentations will have widest appeal if they focus on how people can make or save money, save time, work more efficiently, streamline their organizations, manage their staff more effectively—those kinds of topics.

Keep in mind that your audience—be it a single prospect or a standing-room-only gathering of corporate executives—cares much less about your expertise than about what your expertise brings to them.

Whether you're delivering a brief report to the board of directors or a keynote speech to a major convention, your challenge is to convert your expertise into information that audience members find useful. You will retain their attention only so long as you stay tuned to their station, WII-FM (What's In It For Me?).

"Leave Behinds"

More goes into the preparation process than just selecting the right audience and topics. You need to come up with the right marketing materials to accompany your presentation.

Make sure each audience member walks away with information on how to contact you and take advantage of your services. Supply that information by way of a personal promotion "one-sheet," a brochure, a newsletter, a handout summarizing the key points of your talk, a simple marketing kit, etc.

Tape Yourself

You, too, should walk away with something from your presentation: a tape. Try to tape your talks.

Use an audio- or videotape of your speech as a learning tool to help you improve your style and content.

You can also use the tape as a marketing tool. Send copies to clients, stockholders, the board of directors, the media, or anyone else you want to impress. Your prospects spend more time commuting than ever before. Why not communicate with them through your audiocassette tapes as they commute?

Platform Payment

There's money to be made from speaking—more than $50,000 per presentation if you are a former U.S. president (like Ronald Reagan, immediately after he left office), a decorated military general (like Norman Schwarzkopf, in the aftermath of the Gulf War), or some other major celebrity. Lacking that celebrity status, part-time speakers appearing at corporate meetings or association conferences can expect compensation in the $500-$2500 range.

If you're not an established speaker or author, or a big name in your field, there may be no compensation at all. Don't expect a check when you address a routine meeting of a trade group or community organization. The payoff is in the exposure and the resulting spinoff business opportunities.

Speaking Profits without Pay

A "no fee" speech need not be a free speech. You can offer your services as a paid consultant to those in your audience who approach you following the presentation.

The more you speak, and the more effectively you present your message, the more often audience members will approach you afterwards. Their backgrounds will vary, but their question will be the same: How can they apply your principles to their situation?

You can assume you have touched those who pose such a question. Chances are they would pay for the privilege of conferring with you privately.

Consulting is a natural and lucrative spinoff from public speaking. People often attach a high value to face-to-face time with an expert. How much you receive for your consulting services will depend on how well you package those services. Most professional consultants charge more than $100 an hour—often, considerably more.

Step #1 in creating a spinoff consulting business is to promote yourself *as* a consultant. That means including in your handouts a flyer promoting your services. It means sharing information about those services with the individual who introduces you. And it means mentioning, during your presentation, your availability as a consultant.

One additional opportunity for income at a free speech: product sales. Use your speeches to sell books, tapes, or other products you have developed. Professional speakers can double their income from back-of-the room sales. You can at least *add* to yours.

It doesn't take much to come up with salable products. Record your presentations, and make the tapes available for sale. Create "how to" or "do and don't" lists on laminated cards, and sell them. Laminated topic summary cards, highlighting the key points in your presentation, can also be money makers.

* * * * *

Speaking and free publicity represent smart marketing at its best. Learn to master these two strategies, and you may never again need to pay to promote yourself.

Action Ideas and Tips

251 **Write news releases.** Submit a release to a trade magazine or in-house publication each time you sign a key contract, break a sales record, win an award, or receive other recognition.

252 **Write articles.** Submit an article to a trade or general publication on problems in your industry and your proposed solutions to them. Distribute reprints of the published story to clients and others you seek to influence.

253 **Recycle your articles.** Develop similar articles for several trade publications. Customize them for each publication by inserting quotes, anecdotes, case studies and examples relevant to the readers of that publication.

254 **Distribute your news in the neighborhood.** Start with local and regional business media. Contact the local "Business Journal" publication(s) in your area, and other regional business media with news about yourself and your organization. Those publications are more likely than general news media to carry your story.

255 **Write letters to the editor.** Send them to publications that your target audience reads. Comment on issues related to your industry:

Express concern or outrage, expose a problem or scandal, cite a controversy, gloat over good news, make a prediction, discuss trends, etc.

256 **Deliver the data.** To increase your chances that the media will run your story, provide a fact sheet about the topic, a chronology of key events related to it, and a list of other information sources.

257 **Promote your publicity.** Once a story by or about you appears in the media, promote the fact. Send out e-mail messages, press releases, and personal notes, and add a note to your Web page and other promotional material explaining how you have been featured in the media.

258 **Become a columnist.** Offer to write a column on your area of expertise for a regional or national trade or general publication. Ask that the column include your photograph and biographical information.

259 **Let the newsletters know.** Send copies of your articles to newsletters in your field. Offer the editors permission to reprint them for a fee or for the commitment to run promotional information about you.

260 **If at first you don't succeed...** Should a publication reject your article, offer to make yourself available for an interview on the topic. Submit additional information that a staff writer can use for an article.

261 **Get written about.** Convince a publication to write an article *about* you. Pitch your story idea to the appropriate editor or reporter, and follow up with a press release and photograph. Provide complete background information about yourself and your organization.

262 **Meet the messengers.** Make appointments with reporters or editors to deliver your release and other information in person. Offer to take them to coffee or lunch. Get to know them, and find out more about their future information needs.

263 **Be rapid with your releases.** If a publication or broadcast outlet requests that you *send* your release, do so by fax or e-mail as soon as possible. Mailing your information makes it appear less timely and less important.

264 **Make your releases retrievable.** Post news releases on your Web site, distribute them via e-mail and send them to appropriate newsgroups. The releases can be "archived" on the Web server so others can refer to them in the future.

265 **Be tactful in your "trackdown."** If your information doesn't appear in print, follow up tactfully with reporters. Ask them if they desire "additional information" for your release. That's a better way of jogging their memories than asking if they received the release (a question some of them resent).

266 **Consider a clipping service.** Tracking down whether your release was used becomes more difficult if you have sent it to publications outside your local area. One option: Consult clipping services listed in the Yellow Pages, such as Bacon's Clipping Bureau (800-621-0561).

267 **Contact the media with "show and tell" information.** You can make news every time you:
- introduce a new product or service
- receive a promotion
- win an award
- add a new client
- complete a key project
- participate in a professional conference
- contribute to a charity
- hire an employee
- relocate your office

268 **Contact the media with information related to today's news.** Explain, for example, how your company, your industry, or your area is affected by a breaking story.

269 **Contact the media with tips:** Examples:
- how to make money
- how to save money

- how to save time
- how to run a business, motivate employees, etc.
- how to improve customer service

270 **Contact the media with surveys, opinions, and analyses.** Examples:
- trends in your industry
- survey of individuals or companies in your field
- your predictions
- poll of customers' views of products, services

271 **"Time" negative news.** If you have to make a public confession, or deliver sensitive or embarrassing news in the media, Friday is the day to do so. That's because the information likely will appear in print and on the air on Saturday, a day when most people pay more attention to weekend activities than to the news.

272 **Turn your article into an event.** After you write an article, contact an organization that it directly affects. Suggest the organization host an event at which you deliver a speech on the topic (e.g., *If you write on weatherproofing your home, contact a local public utility company about sponsoring your presentation on the topic*).

273 **Get your products profiled.** Send tapes, booklets, and any of your other educational products to trade publications, and invite the editors to review them.

274 **Donate to the drives.** Contribute autographed copies of your books or other products to TV and radio fundraising drives. Make them available to book fairs, or book and author lunches sponsored by charitable organizations.

275 **Get groups to talk up your talks.** Enlist the groups to which you speak in your publicity efforts. Have them distribute "preview" and "review" news releases to local and trade media before and after your presentation.

276 **Send transcripts to the trades.** Provide trade or in-house publications with written transcripts of your speeches. Include any information the staff can use to write an article about the topic—and you. Make yourself available for an interview on the topic.

277 **Speak for your organization.** If you work for a large organization, announce your interest in speaking in its behalf. Provide a list of your topics and other personal background material.

278 **Speak for your trade association.** Offer your services at conferences and other events put on by trade associations in your field. Get in touch with the associations' regional or state affiliates. Also contact the national offices about presenting to affiliates nationwide.

279 **Get a sponsor.** Prior to your speech, contact an organization eager to reach the same audience you will address. Offer to promote their products during or after your speech in return for their financial support.

NOTE: Get the host organization's approval before approaching a sponsor. Some organizations discourage or prohibit speaker sponsorship.

280 **Hone your speaking skills.** To put on a peak performance:
(1) Practice with a video- or tape-recorder and rehearse in front of family or staff.
(2) Memorize your opening so you can maintain eye contact at the outset.
(3) Tell stories; use visuals to make information interesting. Do something unusual every three minutes.
(4) Show flair and energy.
(5) End with a grand finale. Send them out laughing, thinking, and saying yes.
—*Power Speak* by Dorothy Leads

281 **Watch what you eat before you speak.** Steer clear of the following prior to a presentation:
• cold or caffeinated drinks (Both can cause vocal cord contraction and hoarseness. A healthier alternative: water at room temperature.)
• dairy products, which can cause phlegm buildup
• greasy foods, a source for acid indigestion

282 **Visual-ize success.** Visuals can turn a good presentation into a great one. Studies show that:
• Retention increases 14–38% when listeners see something as well as hear it.
• Speakers' goals are met 34% more often when visuals are used than when visuals aren't.
• Group consensus occurs 21% more often in meetings with visuals than without.
• Time required to present a concept can be reduced up to 40% with the use of visuals.
Visuals can enliven a dull topic, boost your credibility, and enable you to cover more information in less time.
—*You've Got to Be Believed to Be Heard* by Bert Decker

283 **Customize, localize, and personalize.** Distribute prepresentation questionnaires to meeting planners. Ask about the key challenges, "hot buttons," and issues confronting the group you will be addressing. Interview at least six group members and quote them freely in your presentation.

284 **Fill the seats with VIPs.** Invite key clients and prospects, media representatives, and others you seek to influence to your presentation. Ask the host organization to invite other groups, thereby assuring you of a larger turnout—and more potential for self-promotion.

285 **Go back to school.** Offer to speak at school assemblies and classes, if your expertise is relevant to younger audiences. Encourage students to pass on your information—and handouts—to their parents.

286 Help them help their customers. Approach a bank, office supply store, insurance agency or other establishment about offering your program as a service to their customers. Contact your best customers with the same idea.

Offer to present a program for the staff or customers of a prospective client, or the trade association to which the prospect belongs.

287 Let your materials do the talking. Distribute promotional material at every speaking engagement. Include a complete list of your products and services and other background information.

288 Invite feedback. Include an evaluation form soliciting feedback, testimonials, and speaking and general business referrals.

289 Hold onto your audience. Other ways to collect names of those who attend your presentations:
- Distribute a sign-in sheet.
- Collect business cards for a door-prize drawing. Donate your consultation time, or tapes, booklets or other educational tools as the prizes.
- Request a mailing list from the sponsoring organization.

290 Have your talk taped. Suggest that the host group record your presentation and provide it to members unable to attend. Obtain a copy for your own promotional purposes.

Recommend that the group photograph you for use in its newsletter article recapping the speech. Request copies of the photos, again, for your promotional purposes.

291 Use tapes as promotional tools. Distribute them to clients, prospects, the media—and to other organizations that use outside speakers.

292 Ask the host group for help. Request:
- advertising or article space in its publication
- an opportunity to enclose your flyer in its next mailing
- free booth space, if there's a conference exhibit area

293 Join the talk show circuit. Offer to be a guest on TV and radio talk shows, and public-access programs on local cable channels. Watch the shows ahead of time to determine their format, themes, etc. Then contact a show's producer after a daily broadcast with a topic that affects health, heart, home, or pocketbook.

294 Make your pitch in print. Follow your call with a letter outlining the topics you want to discuss. Cite your previous experience on shows and include your media kit and other promotional material.

295 **Suggest a local angle for a national story.** When you contact talk show producers, tie your topic into national stories. Examples: if you're a teacher or counselor, suggest a program about the impact on local children of a national tragedy; if you're an insurance agent or builder, explain how you could provide local home-owners with tips on how to protect their property, etc.

296 **Make your topic timely.** Try, for example, to connect it with an upcoming holiday. Restaurateurs can offer Thanksgiving recipes, store owners can unveil hot Xmas gifts, florists can discuss what's hot for Valentines Day, etc.

297 **Write your own interview questions.** Once you're booked on a talk show, supply the host with a list of 10 pertinent questions. Often, the host will use them word for word, and thank you for your legwork. Prepare at least three "commercials" you intend to get in no matter what happens.

298 **Connect with the producers.** Good resources to help you contact producers:
- "The Top 200 TV Report" (800-669-0773), a listing of the top 200 TV shows that do interviews. Includes producer names, phone numbers and tips on how to pitch them.
- "Top National TV Talk Shows" (800-989-1400), a rundown on program listings for all major TV talk shows. Includes producer

names, phone numbers, beats and show profiles.
- "How to Get on Radio Talk Shows All Across America Without Leaving Your Home or Office" (303-722-7200), a list of names, numbers, and other information to get on radio talk shows.

299 **Connect with the camera.** In preparing for a TV interview:
- wear medium colors (blue, green, maroon, wine, light brown, russet, gold, dark gray)
- avoid wearing solid white or black
- avoid wearing a striped or patterned shirt or blouse
- accessorize: women with belts, jackets, scarves and small jewelry; men with belts, ties, jackets and suspenders
- wear translucent face powder to kill any shine from lights

300 **Get a dub.** Following a TV appearance, obtain a videotape copy for future marketing. For taped radio or TV appearances, take a blank cassette to the station before your segment is going to air and ask the producer to do a dub for you. The tapes can serve as demos when you apply for future opportunities.
Follow up with thank-you notes to the writers, editors, producers, talk show hosts, etc.
—*Getting Business to Come to You* by Paul and Sarah Edwards and Laura Clampitt

CHAPTER SEVEN

Get in Touch

"Who you know is more important that what you know."
—author unknown

"**O**K, team," Coach Knute Rockne was said to have told his Notre Dame football players at the end of a rousing halftime speech, "Go out there and fight, fight, fight!"

His speech could have been addressed to self-promoters as well. We, too, can't get the job done by sitting around the locker room—or behind our desks. We, too, need to get up and out to carry out our missions. We, too, need to get out there and fight, fight, fight!

But *how* do we get out there? How do we make the biggest splash, the greatest impact with our message?

The most effective strategy is to start by prospecting—getting in touch with those we need to influence—and then turning those contacts into contracts.

The best prospectors are the best qualifiers—those self-promoters most skilled at identifying individuals with a need for what they sell, the ability to pay for fulfilling that need, and the motivation and authority to do so.

Set Your Sights

You need to focus on the right prospects. These may include administrators who will determine whether to *retain* your services, chief financial officers who will determine if they can *afford* your services, or executives who will determine whether to *recommend* your services.

Persist in your pursuit of these decision makers, however difficult it is to reach them. Chances are you know the frustration of attempting to bypass the gatekeepers by trying voice mail, e-mail, and everything short of blackmail to reach decision makers who never seem to be available.

> "Reach for the stars. You won't reach them, but you won't come up with a handful of mud, either."
> —Leo Burnett

Try as you will, you may not be able to get around the gatekeeper—that receptionist, secretary, office manager, junior level administrator, or personal assistant whose mission is to deflect as many calls as possible, to save his or her boss the time and effort of dealing with you directly.

Your challenge is to come up with a commercial message and presentation that are so compelling that the gatekeepers *want* to open the gate to the decision makers.

The process is much easier, of course, if decision makers already know and, better yet, support you. How do you get to that stage? Launch a targeted personal promotion campaign in which you distribute the right information about yourself through the right channels to reach the right people. In this chapter, you'll read about several techniques that will ease your access to your top prospects.

Start with Your 5M Plan

First, map out your prospecting plan. That plan should spell out the:
- Mission—your goals (financial and otherwise)
- Message—your personal "commercial"

- Market—who you're trying to reach
- Methods—your personal prospecting strategies
- Measurement—the means by which you'll judge the success of your prospecting efforts

> "You can't hit a target you cannot see, and you cannot see a target you do not have."
> —Zig Ziglar

Market to Your Target

"Target practice" is important here. You need to get ready and take aim before you fire. You need to know what—and who—you're aiming at.

You can waste valuable time, not to mention money and energy, chasing down prospects who can't do you any good. To succeed, narrow your field of prospects to ten at a time. Select the ten who offer the greatest benefits to you right now.

That's a formidable task, considering all of the prospects you encounter through personal contact, the Internet, business associations, and elsewhere. Your job is to separate out the cream of the crop.

Qualify Your Prospects

Put your investigative skills to use. Gather enough information to qualify—and disqualify—those on your prospect list. Your mission is to identify those who would make the best long-term customers. Then zero in on those who exert the most influence, and those who control the budget and can pay you the kind of money you need to reach your financial goals.

Part of the "zeroing in" process involves asking the right questions. Art Sobczak, a telephone sales specialist, contends that the most successful sales professionals are "master questioners." They identify and unlock the needs, concerns, and desires of their prospects, then "move them into a state of mind where they begin wanting a product or service like yours—even before you begin presenting it."

To qualify your prospects, you need answers to some basic questions about your prospects—questions like: What are their goals? What are their problems? What is their pain?

You must identify whether they have a need for what you have to offer, the ability to pay for it, and a commitment not only to buy it—but to buy it *now*. And, you need to know if they alone are authorized to make the buying decision.

If you're dissatisfied with the answers to your qualifying questions, move on and turn your attention elsewhere.

Reach Out and Touch Your Prospects

Get to know the best ways to reach your prospects. Some suggestions:

Find out what publications they read. Learn how to write for those publications—and how to get written about in those publications. A published article not only gets your name in front of your prospects, it also conveys the message that you are an acknowledged expert in your field.

Identify the groups to which your prospects belong. Consider becoming involved with, and speaking before, those groups.

Customize your message and materials to relate directly to your prospects. That means learning their language and incorporating it into your own.

Do Your Homework!

Good prospecting takes good market research. Start your research by checking on your competitors. You can often find out about their activities from trade associations and trade publications.

To learn more about those competitors, call anonymously (or have someone else do so), and get on their mailing lists. Request copies of their sales brochures and annual reports. You can also talk to their suppliers and clients and check out their Web sites.

You can gather information about your hottest prospects by conducting a survey.

Tie your survey questions to events or stories in the day's news that would be relevant to your prospects. That adds timeliness and credibility to your calls, and also helps to break the ice. And it gives you an excuse for calling *today.*

Ask corporate executives to predict what lies ahead for their companies. Question chief financial officers about future spending plans. Survey product development specialists on how they adapt to the changing marketplace. Call on sales managers to share their biggest pet peeves.

Distribute the survey by regular mail, e-mail, telephone, fax—or hand deliver it. Inform your survey respondents that you will send them the results. Remind them of the potential benefits of this up-to-date industry information.

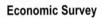

Economic Survey

Over the next six months, do you expect....

1. your staff to increase, decrease, or remain the same ?

2. to buy any new vehicles?

3. to implement a new marketing effort?

4. to buy any new computer equipment?

Should the article then appear in print, distribute copies to those that you contacted. It could open up some important doors for you.

And if the survey doesn't make it into print? Publish the results yourself. Write a summary of your findings, complete with graphs and tables. Put a cover on it that includes your name and phone number, and send your report to your prospects. Send *that* to trade publications and local media—even if they turned down your earlier article.

Once your survey results get published, you become an industry expert who will be called on by prospects and media.

Include a thank-you note along with the article reprint or report that you distribute to prospects. That will get your name in front of them and make it easier for you to get them on the phone or otherwise approach them in the future. So will the additional credibility you will have as the author of a published survey.

Online Promotion

If you want your message to be instantly accessible to millions of people, there's simply no better way than the Internet to promote yourself.

One of the best ways to broadcast your message online is through a Web site. That site can serve as your personal corporate headquarters on the Internet and your electronic billboard in cyberspace.

An effective Web site creates an online identity by which you can hold your own against larger and longer-established competitors. Just like them, you can use your site to provide complete information about yourself, your products, and your services.

Think of a Web site as your master marketing file. You can include brochures, catalogs, articles, product and service lists, customer lists, testimonials, flyers and much more.

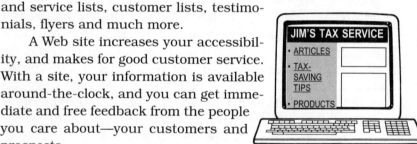

A Web site increases your accessibility, and makes for good customer service. With a site, your information is available around-the-clock, and you can get immediate and free feedback from the people you care about—your customers and prospects.

Winning Web Pages

Whether you create your own Web page, or hire someone to create it for you, heed these suggestions from Internet expert David E. Gumpert, a former editor of the *Harvard Business Review* and *Inc.* magazine:

- Make your page credible.
- Update your materials.
- Involve your "visitors."
- Promote your page.

Gumpert, the president of Net-Marquee Online Services, a Needham, Massachusetts provider of content for use on the Internet, advises against "inordinately self-serving" language on your page.

"Net-iquette," he says, discourages "excessively promotional" claims on your page and, particularly, in the newsgroup and commercial service forums you use to draw attention to your page.

Focus, instead, on providing valuable free information. When you send e-mail responses to those who request your information, you can promote yourself more aggressively.

Adding Power to Your "Page"

Keep your page timely by regularly updating it. That gives visitors a reason to return often. Provide results of a survey, bit by bit on a week-by-week basis. Run a contest. Publish a series of articles over an extended period.

"Online game shows, trivia contests, and the like are the way to get people to register at your site and tell you their interests."
—Seth Godin, *e-Marketing*

It's easy to insert on-screen order forms and information about new products and customer support services. Add new articles and fresh information about your industry as well as about yourself. Provide new links to databases, or new color images, pictures, and text.

Gumpert recommends interacting with those who visit your Web page—through discussion forums, e-mail alerts about new content, and other means. Poll your customers and get their feedback on various topics. You can even test market new product ideas on the "Net" and get instant evaluations.

Promote Your Web Site

Finally, get the word out about your Web site every way you can. Remember, Web-based marketing and sales is reactive. You need to *attract* those you seek to influence. They're not likely to show up at your Web page on their own. Try media releases, e-mail, and newsgroup messages. And add your Web-page address to all of your promotional materials.

List your page with commercial search engines like WebCrawler and Yahoo. You can also pay other services to list your Web address in hundreds of locations.

Newsgroups provide you with a means to mass market information about your Web page. Join a newsgroup, create an online identity, and use e-mail to respond to questions about yourself, your business, and your industry.

Take advantage of your group membership by soliciting feedback and information from others. That feedback becomes especially valuable when you receive an endorsement from a group member who has used your products or services.

By 1997, there were about 20,000 newsgroups, covering a wide range of commercial, academic, recreational, and other topics. You can narrow down your list by reviewing group charters, their message traffic, and the answers included in their "Frequently Asked Questions" (FAQs) sections.

Fusion Marketing

It's worth your while to align with professionals in related fields, and explore joint promotions to prospects. Airlines, rental car companies, and hotels practice this on a grand scale. Rent a car or stay in a hotel, and you get airline points.

> FUSION MARKETING: "Combining the efforts of two entities to 'explode' their joint marketing effectiveness."
> —Jay Conrad Levinson, the *Guerrilla Marketing* series

Cooperative marketing is just as apparent on the local level. Buy a rug at an area carpet dealer, and they hand you a coupon for a local carpet cleaning service. Visit the cleaning service, and you walk out with a coupon for the dealership.

Successful sales professionals recognize the wisdom of joining forces with their suppliers and manufacturers' reps. The joint marketing effort enables the sales pros to secure underwriting for their marketing and promotion.

With whom can you join forces? Think about what would benefit your customers, and what types of businesses could generate good prospects for you.

You can also cross-promote within your broad area of expertise. For example, if you are a real estate lawyer who is approached with a divorce question, contact a

Fusion Marketing Circus-Style

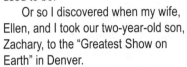

Going to the circus certainly ain't what it used to be.

Or so I discovered when my wife, Ellen, and I took our two-year-old son, Zachary, to the "Greatest Show on Earth" in Denver.

The circus, itself, is still way cool. They still shoot the clown out of the cannon, propelling him from one end of the tent to the other. The acrobats still do their astounding flips high above the crowd. The elephants still stand on their hind legs, and the lions and tigers still jump through flaming hoops.

But going to the circus, I discovered, sure has changed.

Maybe because the popcorn and cotton candy, which used to come in a box and on a stick, respectively, and cost next to nothing, are now available in commemorative buckets for about $10 each.

Maybe because representatives now aggressively hawk the circus' online store, and clowns peddle a special Circus MasterCard during intermission.

Or maybe because of the Sears factor: the Sears coupons in the circus program, the Sears signs and banners around the coliseum, and the Sears representatives on hand as you enter.

Why Sears?

Very simply, because the Ringling Bros. and Barnum & Bailey Circus is now brought to you by Sears.

A little bit of fusion marketing under the Big Top—and at the hardware store.

divorce attorney. Encourage him or her to refer future real estate problems to you in exchange for divorce case referrals. Cross-referrals help your customers get what they want, and bring you new customers.

Customer Input Can Boost Your Output

When it comes to prospecting and promotional activities, you need not go it alone. Call on your customers for help.

Try hosting a dinner or other customer appreciation event for your best clients, and use the occasion to:

(1) Express your thanks for their patronage.

(2) Seek their input on how to expand your business.

You can accomplish that second objective simply by stating the Master Marketer's Four Magical Words:

"I NEED YOUR HELP."

Some of your most useful marketing and prospecting ideas will come out of customer focus groups. Your best customers are your biggest fans. You'll find them very forthcoming with prospecting ideas.

You can also use appreciation events to inform customers of your newest products and services, and to ask them for referrals.

Focus groups with former customers are also worthwhile. You can gather prospecting suggestions from them as well as find out why they stopped working with you. Reuniting with ex-clients in a focus group can help you reopen the lines of communication.

Another type of focus group is a personal board of advisors. Invite professionals whom you know and respect, and who are well-attuned to the local business scene. I attended one of these focus group sessions with Jeffrey Davidson, a business consultant, author, and professional speaker. On hand were about 25 business professionals: a mix of lawyers, journalists, doctors, CEOs, and entrepreneurial business owners.

After he served us dinner, he pulled out a cassette tape recorder and called on us to share our thoughts. And share we did, so much so that Davidson emerged with a few audiocassettes of invaluable tips on how to attract additional prospects.

"Warm Calls"

There are a number of ways you can warm up those cold prospecting calls. Referrals from customers and others make your job a lot easier. It's in your best interest to get and follow up on as many referred leads as possible.

Your calls to prospects take on a special significance when a third-party letter of introduction precedes them. Ask influential individuals whom you know to write letters on your behalf to influential people *they* know.

The letter should emphasize the importance of your upcoming call. The letter should praise you, and recount some of the career-enhancing, life changing, or other benefits you have provided the writer.

Write Your Own Referral Letters

Perhaps you don't know many professionals with the time, inclination, or creativity to write a referral letter. That's when you should offer to write the letter yourself.

Write the letter yourself? Why, sure! Remember: No one can promote you as well as you. Seize the opportunity to write your own letters of introduction. Put your words, extolling you and what you stand for, in the mouths and on the letterhead of others, for reproduction on their letterhead.

Submit your draft to them for their review and approval, after which they can reproduce it on their letterhead.

Testimonials

Quality Letter, Quality Paper
A good testimonial letter belongs on good quality letterhead. Forego cheap copies in favor of reproduction of your letter on the company's actual stationery. Request extra copies of their testimonial letter on their actual letterhead.

Use the same system with testimonial letters. It's easy to convince those you've served to let you write your testimonial letter. The key, again, is to submit it for their approval.

Some of the most glowing letters ever written about leading professionals have been written *by* those professionals.

Testimonial letters that make the greatest impact cover the benefits of your services, explain how clients benefit from them, and how much they trust you. Words from others are many times more effective than anything you could say about yourself.

Making Your "Net" Work

Networking skills are a prerequisite for effective self-promotion.

From Bob Burg, a networking specialist and professional speaker, come these "10 Tips for Effective Networking":

(1) Focus on meeting "Center of Influence" people.

(2) Invest 99 percent of a first-time conversation with a networking prospect on asking questions about that person's business.

(3) Questions should be open-ended so that they can't be answered with "yes" or "no."

(4) Focus on the best question you can ask: "What can I do if somebody I'm talking to would be a good prospect for you?"

(5) Get their business cards.

(6) Send a handwritten thank-you note that day.

(7) Send reprints of articles that would interest your networking prospects.

(8) Send something monthly to keep you on their minds.

(9) Send leads.

(10) Send a handwritten thank-you note whenever you receive a lead.

Don't wait until you need clients to practice your networking skills. Reach out and connect with those you seek to influence *before* you have to. Develop a high profile and build relationships. These relationships will protect you in future times of need, and bolster your success.

Seek out those who have gone successfully before you. Network with veterans in your field who can advise you on promotion and prospecting strategies that worked for them—and on those that didn't.

> "All purchase decisions, all repurchase decisions, hinge, ultimately, on conversations and relationships....All dealings are personal dealings in the end."
> —Tom Peters

Prospecting at Trade Shows

Trade shows can be a networking and prospecting paradise.

The book *Guerrilla Trade Show Selling* points out that shows enable you to:
- sell what you offer to visitors
- sell what you offer to other exhibitors
- accumulate leads for your sales force to pursue
- network and troubleshoot with other professionals

Trade show demonstrations can differentiate your product and, according to studies, increase the comprehension of your message by 65 percent. They can help you highlight product features, dramatize a product's problem-solving capabilities, and reduce fear of change related to a product.

Use trade shows to work the crowd as well as, or instead of, your booth. Distribute (and collect) as many business cards as possible.

Some Final Notes

Clearly it's important to make a good impression when you get in touch with your prospects. It's equally important to maintain that good impression if you intend to *stay* in touch with them.

In selecting your prospecting strategy of choice, a simple rule of thumb is to do what your competitors don't. Focus on those prospects you need to influence and make contact.

Action Ideas and Tips

301 **Talk up your target groups.** Once you've decided on the target group(s) for your prospecting, announce the fact in press releases to general or trade media. Explain how you'll "specialize" by providing your services to the group(s).

302 **Put catalogs to work for you.** Get listed in directories published by the nation's nearly 4,000 catalog companies. Send your background information along with a product flyer, news release and photo.

For lists of catalog companies, consult the following sources:

- *The National Directory of Catalogues* (Oxbridge Communications: 212-741-0231)
- *Standard Rate & Data Service (SRDS)*, the publisher of a list of major mail houses and mailers (708-574-6000)
- *Catalogue Solutions,* an agent which helps you contact catalog producers for about 10% of sales (Jess Clarke; 203-454-1919)

—Ted Nicholas, publisher, *Direct Marketing Success Letter*

303 **Find a mentor in your industry.** Offer to help him or her in exchange for advice on how you can promote yourself and achieve your goals. Or, simply take movers and shakers to lunch and seek their self-promotion recommendations.

304 **Team up.** Explore joint promotion possibilities with a noncompeting firm. Launch publicity campaigns together and share the cost of printing, mailing, and such reference tools as media directories. Cosponsor promotional events and cooperate in other ways—such as sharing mailing lists and leads.

305 **Promote the partnership idea.** Establish allied professionals as a target group for your marketing. Write for, speak to, or network with trade groups and discuss your interest in sharing leads and referrals with their group members.

306 **Keep your Web site current.** Offer contests, giveaways, and personalized accounts of timely events (e.g., business conferences or trade shows). Run an "Ask the Expert" feature that responds to questions posed by visitors to your site.

307 **Promote your page.** List your home page and e-mail addresses within all of your other marketing materials. Include them on the following:

- letterhead
- business cards
- flyers
- brochures
- fax cover sheets

- media kits
- media releases
- promotional giveaways (e.g., mouse pads, pens, calendars, etc.)
- Yellow Pages ads
- newsletters
- call waiting background music and information
  —*Marketing on the Internet* by Matthew and Jill Ellsworth

308 **Promote your page even more.** Other ways to promote your home page: Distribute a flyer to everyone in your database, or launch a mass mailing campaign. Include the information in ads, and in your e-mail messages to the newsgroups or commercial service forums.
—*Marketing on the Internet*

309 **Connect with online newsgroups.** Post a notice offering to answer questions about your specialty. Follow the group's ground rules by asking permission to discuss your business.

310 **Sponsor a page for an event or organization.** Nonprofit groups, public information organizations, and charity events always seek this kind of assistance — and they will acknowledge your efforts on the page. Use the page to provide a "hot" link to your own Web site.

311 **Join or start a networking group.** Start your own "tipster" group, a lead-sharing organization for individuals in different professions. Or,

join one. If you run your own business, or would like to, join or create a local business executives group.

312 **Create your own "board of directors."** Gather professionals from various fields to help you promote yourself to advance within your career.

313 **Develop a mastermind group.** Organize a group of professionals in your field. Share information about new technologies and trends, discuss common challenges, etc.

314 **Exhibit at a trade show.** By getting involved with a trade show, you can:
- visit with people who are otherwise hard to meet
- introduce new products to the market
- find new dealers, representatives and distributors
- find new employees
- scope out the competition
- get media exposure
  —*Guerrilla Trade Show Selling* by Mark S.A. Smith, Orvel Ray Wilson and Jay Conrad Levinson

315 **Capture the moment.** You have precious little time to make an impact at a trade show. According to research by Incomm International:
- 6% of visitors to booths don't wait at all
- 11% wait only 30 seconds
- 41% wait one minute

- 38% wait three minutes
- 14% wait five minutes

316 **Wow 'em with your trade show demonstrations.** Use these techniques to make a lasting impression:
- Focus on no more than three key sales points.
- Stand on a raised platform.
- Involve the audience; let as many as possible hold or use the product.
- Don't hand out brochures until after the demonstration.

317 **Time your follow-ups.** Try to follow up no sooner than, nor later than 48 hours following a trade show. The 48-Hour Rule is the best way to insure that you will be visible and remembered by the prospects when they are still fresh from your meeting, but not overwhelmed by the mail and messages awaiting them upon their return to the office.
—*How to Get the Most Out of Trade Shows* by Steve Miller

318 **Play host.** Connect with movers and shakers by hosting at your office an event for a group to which they belong. Consider chambers of commerce, boards of trade, networking groups for executives, service clubs, and other groups.

319 **Punch up your prospecting letters.** Stress the prospect's needs and how you can satisfy them. Avoid the overused "I can do all this, call-me-if-you-need-me" approach.

Include a summary of the problem, a solution to that problem, accounts of others who have benefited from your services, a "next step," and a "P.S." that repeats a key point or offers an additional benefit.

320 **Tempt them to open the envelope.** Increase the chances the envelope will be opened by including the words "private" or "confidential," and by omitting your name and address.

321 **Make a prospecting plan.** Pinpoint action objectives each time you call a prospect.
Some ideas for customer-action objectives:
- to get a referral from the prospect
- to have the prospect arrange for a meeting with other decision makers
- to convince the prospect to try a new product sample
- to convince the prospect to buy what you're selling
—*Value-Added Selling Techniques* by Tom Reilly

322 **Be a problem solver.** Drop notes to prospects with suggestions on how they can resolve a problem. Recommend a meeting to discuss problems.
—*Career Power* by Richard Rinella and Claire Robbins

323 **Promote yourself in person.** It's hardest for someone to say no to your face, easier to say no to your voice, and easiest to say no to your letter.

It's much more difficult to close a sale on the phone than in person. You typically reach five in 20 prospects you call, and sell to one in 20 prospects you reach.

324 **Call between 9 and 10 a.m.— their time.** That's the period designated by the American Telemarketing Association as "the Golden Selling Hour."

325 **Call early or late in the day.** If you can't connect with a decision maker, try calling before 9 a.m. or after 5 p.m. You're less likely to encounter a gatekeeper.

326 **Call early—or late—in the week.** Call on Monday or Friday, and you'll avoid the midweek crush of sales calls. Monday's calls catch your prospects as they plan the week ahead. Friday's calls enable you to reach prospects as they think about the following week.
—*10 Secrets of Marketing Success*

327 **First tell how you help, then what you do.** Give top priority to your benefits when calling a prospect. Tell how you help clients make or save money, save time, increase productivity, solve problems, etc.

328 **Leave voice mail messages that matter.** Include the reason for your call, rather than just your name and number.

- Include a few questions for which you need answers, and any other information that will prepare them for your next conversation.
- Repeat your name and number at the end of your message, to save them rewinding time.
—*Guerrilla Selling* by Jay Conrad Levinson, Bill Gallagher, and Orvel Ray Wilson

329 **Make voice mail appointments.** Inform prospects that you will call back at 4 p.m.—or that they can reach you at 9:30 a.m. tomorrow. Or that you can "stop by" Tuesday. Follow up with a fax or e-mail note confirming the message.

330 **When you get feedback, get referrals.** When you send evaluation forms to customers, ask for names of potential prospects. The more space you leave for referrals, the more you'll receive.

331 **Ask customers to talk up your company.** Offer to send them a gift for every customer who mentions them.
—*Guerrilla Marketing Weapons* by Jay Conrad Levinson

332 **Personalize your presentations.** Send questionnaires to top officials at an organization before you speak at their meeting. Ask about key challenges confronting group members. Interview audience members ahead of time, and quote them in your presentation.

333 **Call on clients to call ahead.** Ask them to contact those that they know to promote you and to inform others of your upcoming call or letter.

334 **Word it right.** When following up on a referral, indicate that the individual who referred you "wanted" you to call. That verb works better than "recommended" or "suggested."

335 **Spread the news.** Call prospects with news that affects them. Follow up by sending news articles.

336 **Qualify first.** Find out who in the organization has decision-making and budgetary authority. If possible, ask your contact to call them on your behalf.

337 **Probe your prospects.**

- Have you ever used the kind of services that I offer?

- What would it be worth to you to solve your problems? What would it cost you if you didn't?

- If you did invest in these services, what would have to happen for you to be fully satisfied with them?

338 **Offer more than just a business card.** Use your first meeting to make available, at no cost, a sample, a product trial, a discount coupon, an hour consultation, a needs analysis, a book, tape, or article—or some other incentive for contacting you.

339 **Use "call for action words."** Try these words to encourage quick response:

- Limited time offer
- Time is running out
- While they last
- Limited availability
- Order before ____
- Introductory offer
- Exclusive offer
- Early bird bonus

340 **"Network" with your body.** In networking, *how* you say it means as much or more that *what* you say. Follow this "ENGAGE" formula:
  E ye contact
  N od
  Grin
  A im your attention
  Gesture appropriately
  E asy posture

341 **Be a networking note-taker.** Take time at networking events to jot down a few notes on the back of each business card you collect. Attach a grade to each card, rating the likelihood of future business.

342 **Don't let a day go by.** Follow up your first meeting with a prospect within 24 hours. Call or send an e-mail message or personal note. Try to advance your relationship.

343 **Be reachable.** The most profitable "prospectors" are available all day, every day, around the clock. Make it easier for your prospects to get in touch with you. Consider a cellular phone, a toll-free number, a pager, call forwarding, three-way calling, an upgraded voice mail system—whatever telephone technology works best for you.

344 **Promise help to promising prospects.** Ask for extra copies of their business cards and other marketing pieces that you can distribute. Recontact your prospects within a week with a few leads, even if they're long shots.

345 **Ask questions.** The more questions you ask your prospects, the tighter the bond you'll form with them. Questions benefit you in several ways. They:
- make people feel important
- provide information
- enable you to best highlight your product's strength
- encourage thought processes
- allow people to talk
- provide you direction
- create the "yes" momentum
  —*Selling is a Woman's Game* by Nicki Joy

346 **Get out your good word.** Provide your prospects with reprints of articles by and about you, new product and service information, a list of resources within your industry, answers to questions they may have about you and your business, etc. You can transmit most of the information via e-mail and fax, but be sure to send handwritten personal notes, too.

347 **Be ready with references.** Be prepared to supply your prospects with a list of names they can consult for more information about you.

Maintain regular contact with those references. Treat them right, and they will play an important role in your personal marketing efforts. Thank them sincerely and often for speaking out in your behalf.

348 **Show references how to refer you.** Sit down with them and recommend words they can use and ways they can respond when a prospect calls about you.

Use the occasion to wine them and dine them, and offer to help *them* in any way you can.

349 **Use your past for prospecting.** Send career updates, photos, and other information to the newspaper in your hometown and to your college alumni publication. Both publications may have influential readers.

350 **Retailer relief.** If you're a retailer, ask manufacturers and wholesalers for help with prospecting and promotion. Ask them for assistance with store displays, advertising, and publicity.

CHAPTER EIGHT

Stay in Touch

"And when he is out of sight, quickly also is he out of mind."
—Thomas Kempis, 15th century German author

I n the realm of personal promotion, no truer words
were ever spoken. You won't get much return for those
exhaustive and exhausting in-person and online prospecting efforts if you don't maintain your contacts.

Perhaps there was a time when there was no need
to stay in touch, when "being good" was all that it took
to achieve success. Become good enough at what you
do, the theory was, and you'll acquire all the fame and
fortune that you could ever need.

That time has passed. Today the competition is too
intense; the field, too crowded; and the technical, economic, and other changes too rapid for us to allow our
careers to run on autopilot.

Control Your Destiny

Those who count on word-of-mouth to guide them
to the top have yielded control of their careers and their
lives to fate. "Que Sera, Sera" is the tune they sing,

trusting that "whatever will be, will be." They have decided to let their careers control them, rather than attempt to control their careers. Whoever calls on them, and whatever services they require, then that is what they provide.

> "Destiny is not a matter of chance, it is a matter of choice; it is not a thing to be waited for, it is a thing to be achieved."
>
> —Williams Jennings Bryan

They are captains of ships without rudders, ships whose ultimate destinations will be determined by the wind and waves and other factors beyond their control.

Self-promoters want more than that. They prefer to control their own destinies to the greatest degree possible. They take a more proactive approach to their success. They know who it is they intend to serve, and how they intend to serve them. They know that staying in touch with the right kind of professionals will move them along the career path of their choosing.

Getting known is only part of your mission as a personal salesperson—perhaps the easiest part. *Staying* known—well, that's something else again.

How well you stay in touch determines how long you stay in business.

"What have you done for me lately?" is on the minds—if not on the lips—of your customers. They expect suitable answers—and substantial proof.

If you snooze, you lose. Fail to communicate with your customers and your competitors will. A customer's tradition with you may not count when a competitor surfaces to fill your customer's need or to solve your customer's problem.

Be a Player

The most successful individuals in any field are those who become "players"—and stay that way. They maintain their visibility and credibility. They demonstrate that they're in the hunt for the long run.

You must maintain and sustain the recognition that you obtain. You must keep in touch with those whom you seek to influence.

> "Your influence is almost directly proportional to the thickness of your Rolodex.™ Work the phone. Don't waste a single lunch. Go to cocktail parties. Who you know is still as important as what you know."
>
>
>
> —Tom Peters

That means networking, and doing what you can to assure that your "net" works over time. It means communicating regularly with the pivotal people in your industry. And it means keeping up with what you need to know, as well as sharing it with *whom* you need to know.

There is both value and challenge in getting referrals, testimonials, and other marketing assistance from those you now serve.

Obvious Value

The value is in the validation and endorsement clients provide when they write kind words on your behalf, or allow you to use their names when approaching others. By doing so, they provide assurances that you are worth listening to. Those assurances help establish your identity, provide you with much-needed name recognition and warm up the coldest of calls.

The Challenge

The challenge posed by referrals and testimonials is that they don't often land in your lap. Usually, they require some effort—effort which comes naturally for seasoned self-promoters. Follow-up is crucial, too.

Your relationship with a client or mentor could deteriorate if you fail to follow up on a referral with a thank-you note, a gift, or a favor in return.

Visible = Viable

Only you can determine the best audience for your message, and the best buyers for your products and services. Once you do, you must stay in front of them. They will perceive your company as viable only so long as you remain visible.

There are many ways to keep the lines of communication open with those you need influence. Personal inquiries, referrals and other business-building leads,

FYI articles, product updates—there are numerous ways you can stay in touch.

Some self-promoters prefer the "up close and personal approach" with prospects and clients.

They ask lots of questions and make lots of references to the personal lives of those they seek to influence. They are quick to recognize birthdays, anniversaries, graduations, and promotions, along with hobbies and outside interests.

Realtors are known for pursuing this personal approach with their prospects.

Your "strictly personal" call will be appreciated, but will it be remembered? Perhaps not, at a time when so many other salespeople and entrepreneurs make similar calls so often. You'll make more of a lasting impact if you can also educate your prospects.

It takes time for you to stay in touch with key prospects and customers—their time as well as yours. It takes time for them to respond to your calls, review your e-mail messages and other communication—time they may not have.

It is your challenge and responsibility to make the best use of their time by providing them with insights and information that will help them achieve their goals.

High Tech, High Touch

Professionals who are most adept at staying in touch—and turning contacts into contracts—rely on various technologies to do so.

A 1996 *Inc.* magazine survey indicated that a whopping 82 percent of the businesses polled expressed confidence in

---

Happy to Hear From You

To make prospects and customers *really* glad you called, offer:
- product updates
- feedback questions ("how'd we do?")
- additional uses and benefits of your product/service
- maintenance/use tips for your product/service
- referrals and leads for their company
- other ideas on how they can increase their business
- free service calls
- discount coupons for future service
- discount coupons for service with an allied company
- invitations to customer appreciation events
- "hotline" accessibility

the payoff of such technologies. These included the Internet, CD-ROM multimedia, laptops, and networks—particularly in the areas of customer service, marketing and product development.

There are many technologies you can use to keep in touch. You can use computer bulletin boards one month, multimedia presentations the next month, video teleconferencing another month, and audio text, fax-on-demand, infomercials, CD-ROM, high-tech "couponing," and point-of-sale computer kiosks in future months.

There are many ways to get help in communicating with your target market. One way is to promote yourself in cooperation with individuals from related, but noncompeting fields. Maintain these relationships and regularly reward your allies, and they will go out of their way to give you additional exposure in the future.

E-mail

When it comes to staying in touch online, one of your best bets is e-mail. E-mail use is big and getting bigger. A Cambridge, Massachusetts market research firm estimates that half the U.S. population was using e-mail by the year 2001—compared to just two percent in 1992.

A well-designed and promoted Web site will attract and get you in touch with the right caliber of prospects. E-mail will *keep* you in touch with those prospects.

Self-promoters are fond of marketing by e-mail because of the latitude it offers. Unencumbered by the restrictions attached to Web page promotion, e-mail users can be more purely promotional and self-serving in their communication. E-mail is, after all, the means by which you can pitch your services to those who respond to your free information offers on your home page and in user groups.

E-mail is a powerful and inexpensive alternative to the telephone. It provides you with access that phone contact does not. The same decision makers who ignore your phone calls may well respond to your e-mail messages.

Adding e-mail to your personal marketing mix enables you to contact large numbers of prospects faster and for less money than you could otherwise. Through e-mail, you can immediately distribute timely information to customers and prospects, post press releases, and keep in touch with online chat and news groups.

In addition, you can customize and personalize your message to a far greater extent on e-mail than through other means.

Another advantage e-mail offers is interactivity, allowing you to give and get feedback from users, prospects, buyers, competitors, and others. It's an international promotional service, through which you can share your message overseas 24 hours a day.

Speed Pays

A hot referral or lead can turn cold if you wait too long to follow up on it.

Staying in touch on a timely basis is the key to maintaining and retaining your customers.

Check in regularly with a prospect or client and time is sure to be on your side. Sooner or later, you'll connect with a company at a time when it needs the kind of services you provide. You may win the contract not necessarily because yours is the best offer— but because it's the *newest* one.

But fall out of touch with those you serve, and you're asking for trouble.

The best kind of follow-up, with the customers you serve as well as the contacts you make, is *instant* follow-up. When you've

"He who hesitates is *last.*"
—Anonymous

"To succeed, jump as quickly at opportunities as you do at conclusions."
—Benjamin Franklin

The Power of Referrals

It had been a long day—too long since the sales trainer had eaten. He had questions—and he hoped the hotel concierge had answers.

"It's late and I'm hungry," he said. "Any suggestions?"

"I've got just what you're looking for," the concierge responded. "Try the 'Rusty Scupper,' down by the waterfront. Great food. Great ambiance. Great location."

And, it turned out, a great big line to get in.

Dejectedly, the trainer took his place at the end of the line that snaked out the door, and along the dock.

It took him 45 minutes to reach the front of the line. The maitre 'd greeted him with a smile and an apology.

"Tell me," the frustrated trainer said. "Is this place always so popular?"

"Well, it's been this way for five weeks now," the maitre 'd replied. "Ever since we held Concierge Night."

just made a contact, follow up immediately while you are still fresh in their minds.

Immediate follow-up makes for good customer relations. Recontact your client within 48 hours of the time you provide a service. You make a positive impression when you call to see if your client is satisfied with your services. It shows that you're there and that you care *after* you delivered the product, or performed the service.

Even if your client is dissatisfied, he or she will appreciate your interest. It's better to find out about and rectify a problem early than to lose the business later on.

Repeat Business Profits

Those you work for or with *now* can be even more valuable to your personal promotion efforts. In marketing, as in sales, your best clients are your *current* clients. Consider the economics: It costs six times less to sell something to a current client than to a prospective one.

Taking a good client to lunch is one of the best ways to nurture your relationship. Think of the return on that $35 (give or take a few bucks, depending on where you dine) investment.

For starters, you can use the meeting to strengthen your bond. Determine if the client is fully satisfied with your services, or seeks improvement in them. If there are concerns, not to worry. You're far better off hearing about them now—and letting your guest vent a bit—than at some later point when he or she recites those concerns as reasons to take the business elsewhere.

Even if they are unhappy, your customers will admire you for taking the time to care. But the odds are that the feedback will be positive. It usually is when you wine and dine and inquire about the well-being of an active client.

Gather Testimonials

Make mental notes of positive remarks from customers. You may be able to use them in future marketing materials, such as testimonial letters for yourself that you end up writing.

How's that? A letter in your behalf that *you* write for a client?

By all means!

In these hectic times, clients often don't have the time to sit down and create an accurate and flattering testimonial letter for you. When confronted with time resistance, offer to perform the task yourself. Advise your clients of your willingness to include their comments about your service in your own version of a letter, then submit it to them for their review.

Should they object to your choice of words, change them until they're satisfied. Once they approve your version, ask them to reproduce the note on their letterhead, and return it to you.

Some of the most glowing, complimentary testimonial letters are in the portfolios of professionals who wrote them themselves. They didn't let something so insignificant as their clients' time constraints stand in the way of terrific testimonials!

Collecting, reproducing, and distributing testimonials can be a time-consuming exercise. But it's an important exercise, if for no other reason than others may note the *absence* of testimonials in your personal portfolio.

Testimonials come in many forms and from many sources. There are the letters others write, those that you write in your own behalf for others, responses to evaluation form questions, remarks scribbled on business cards, and even audio- and videotape versions.

Some testimonial letters even result from contractual commitments, when individuals request them as part of their remuneration.

You can gain more than just good will and a testimonial letter from lunch with a good client. You can gain additional business by inquiring whether they might have additional use for your services in coming months. And your clients can give you the names of others who might benefit from your services.

Referrals

Bill Cates, a personal friend and a fellow professional speaker, contends that referrals can turn business relationships into gold. In his book *Unlimited Referrals*, Cates explains how a referral can turn a routine telephone prospecting effort into a "conversation."

Referrals, he says, provide commonality (the fact that you and your prospect know someone in common) and endorsement. They "turn a cold call into a warm call" and propel you past "voice mail and all the other obstacles to selling."

"Commonality and endorsement don't just make the first conversation easier," Cates writes. "They also significantly increase the chance of the final sale. You'll get fewer obstacles and objections, you'll immediately operate from a higher level of trust, and your new prospect-turned-customer will have a stronger sense of loyalty from the start."

> "Buyers understand what good service is, but they can't hold it in their hands or watch it work before they buy it. This is why meeting you through a colleague or friend is their preferred method. The endorsement and testimony of others make them feel much more comfortable opening their door to you and giving you their business."
> —Bill Cates

Unlimited Referrals cites a Northwestern Mutual Life study of 5,640 prospects indicating that the chances of making a sale were nearly four times greater when the prospecting was done from referrals rather than cold calls.

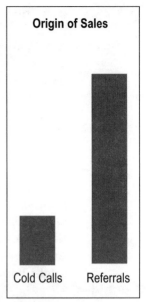

Origin of Sales

Cold Calls   Referrals

Those we have served in the past can help promote us in the future. We need look no further for promotional assistance than the customers, boards of directors, committees, managers, supervisors, associations, trade groups, and others with whom we've worked.

Just because you no longer do business with certain clients doesn't mean you can't *get* business from them. Stay connected with past customers who can assist with your personal promotion efforts.

Prestigious clients with whom you formerly worked can serve as valuable references. They can pave the way for you to penetrate new markets, introduce you to a variety of movers, shakers and heavy hitters, advise you on future market strategies, and assist you in other ways.

It pays to stay on good terms even if you're no longer on their payroll.

Ask your clients for advice on how to reach out to high-caliber prospects. Four of the most useful words you can use with a top client are: "I need your help."

Preface those words with praise and appreciation. Thank the clients for their business, congratulate them on their success, and seek their assistance in advancing your own business.

You may be surprised by how helpful clients can be in advising you on your next moves. Many professionals relish the role of mentor, and will go to great lengths to share ideas on where you should go from here in your personal promotion efforts.

The most useful information comes from the most specific questions. Your best bet is to use phrases like "I'm looking to work with other CEOs like you," or "My

Cultivate Your Sources

Sources have what every self-promoter needs: leads, tips, and news about the industry. Sources come in many varieties: secretaries, office managers, and gatekeepers; trade group representatives; the trade press; vendors, suppliers, and former customers; buyers and purchasing agents who have since joined new firms, and allied professionals—even your competitors. Stay in touch and on good terms with your sources, and you'll stay in touch with your industry.

goal is to expand further into the area of copyright law. What would you suggest?"

You have nothing to lose from seeking the counsel of a top client—and a lot to gain. The best way to get that counsel is through a luncheon appointment.

But don't spend all of your lunch money on clients. Don't forget about sources.

Customer Surveys

There are times when face-to-face, heart-to-heart meetings with your customers aren't feasible. Sometimes you have to rely on a more impersonal alternative: an evaluation form. You can come up with some very useful market research from a written feedback form. Use it to elicit referrals, testimonials (Ask: "What do you think was the most valuable aspect of my service?") and information about future needs for your services.

It's what you don't hear about that can hurt you. The complaint about your service. The concern about your delivery capabilities. The confusion over your catalog. Find out about and address these issues before they turn into serious problems. Head them off before your customers look elsewhere for solutions.

The average business never hears from 96 percent of its unhappy customers, according to the Strategic Planning Institute. But 90 percent or more of those customers will not visit or buy from them again.

The Cambridge, Massachusetts-based research center also reports that for every complaint, the average company has 26 customers with problems. In addition, the average upset customer tells nine people about it, and one in five will tell more than 20.

Unhappy customers usually do you more damage than happy customers do you good. You should attach a high priority to customer service. Clearly, your customers do.

> "Complaints offer companies the opportunity to demonstrate their appreciation of, and interest in, the customer."
> —Janelle Barlow and Claus Møller, *A Complaint Is a Gift*

The fact that you even make an evaluation form available will set you apart from your many competitors who don't follow up in any way.

The written evaluation form lacks the all-important element of personal interaction. Many clients won't take the time to complete and return the form—unless you motivate them to do so. Here's where you need to send a nice gift, or offer some kind of discount off the price of future service.

Make It a Habit to Stay in Touch

Self-promotion in these competitive times is neither a waiting game nor a spectator sport. Those intent on selling themselves don't sit back and wait for favorable word-of-mouth leads to simply come their way. Nor do they watch and see what happens, in hopes that referrals will suddenly materialize.

Rather, they take matters in their own hands. They get and stay in touch with people of influence and they seek out the kind of testimonial endorsements and referrals that will help them meet their quotas and achieve their goals.

Keeping in touch is about persistence and more persistence. You need to keep at it, however many unreturned phone calls, unanswered e-mail messages, and ignored inquiries you may encounter along the way.

Keeping in touch is about self-discipline: developing the motivation and setting aside the time to communicate regularly with key individuals. You can hire staff, public relations professionals, and others to assist you—but, ultimately, you have to do it yourself. You're the one who has to reach out to others and keep listening and keep talking.

None of this energy and commitment would be necessary if you could achieve fame in an instant and maintain it forever. But life isn't like that.

Success doesn't happen overnight. Ever hear that old slogan that it takes "twenty years to become an overnight sensation?" Add to that the idea that it takes a lifetime to *remain* one.

> "We wildly underestimate the power of the tiniest personal touch."
>
> —Tom Peters

Do something, anything to keep your name in front of those you need to know— and who need to know you. The three keys to effective advertising apply here—repetition, repetition, repetition.

In the world of self-promotion, there is no such thing as overkill—but there is such a thing as underexposure. Out of sight really *is* out of mind. Once you disappear, even for a short period, you die.

Action Ideas and Tips

351 **Follow up fast.** In this era of instant communication, tomorrow may be too late for you to follow up. Don't delay in following up on promising leads and contacts. Don't give hot prospects time to cool to your proposals. A quick call, e-mail message, or fax *today* may be all it takes to keep their interest up and your momentum going.

352 **Reward rapid responses.** Your voice mail messages should motivate customers to return your call *now*. Offer discounts if they return your call and place an order by 4 p.m. today. Or offer an extended warranty if they sign the agreement this week.

353 **Reward frequent buyers.** Behavior that gets rewarded gets repeated, so create an awards program for your most consistent customers. Update your customers on new awards, and how close they are to qualifying for them. Keep the motivation high by setting the qualification thresholds low.

354 **Listen for their issues.** Ask the right questions in conversations with key contacts and you'll hear about an issue or topic in which they're especially interested. Make a note of it. It will give you a topic on which you can follow up—and provide an effective ice breaker for your next conversation.

355 **Choose your news.** Each month, determine your most significant recent accomplishments in discussions with those you seek to influence. While you will initiate most of those conversations, you are sure to be asked how *you* are doing. Sharing news about an achievement is more impressive than the boring "I'm doing fine, thanks" response.

356 **Send FYI items.** Small articles can have a large impact. Provide everyone on your mailing list with a copy of each item that appears in a trade or general publication by or about you. Blurbs, stories about contract signings, awards, anniversaries, new hires, volunteer work, etc. make for good FYI material.

357 **Widen your exposure to a narrow niche.** Industry newsletters are your ticket to high visibility within a limited market. Reach out for that exposure through regular news releases, articles, and letters to the newsletter editors.

Consult *Newsletters in Print* by Gale Research in your library. It lists more than 11,000 subscription, membership and free newsletters, bulletins, digests and related publications in the U.S. and Canada.

358 **Promote new technology the old-fashioned way.** Market your Internet presence and Web page as you would any new service—with news releases, marketing materials, etc.

Release your new "address" to trade and general interest publications. List your Web page with a variety of commercial search engines—Web Crawler, Yahoo, and the like.

Post announcements with relevant news groups and bulletin boards. Locating "relevant" ones may take some time since more than 20,000 such sites now exist.

359 **Think links.** Create a list of all the Web pages your prospects might visit, and seek to link them to yours. Realtors might arrange for links with the pages of moving companies. Organic fruit growers might link up with health food stores. Bed-and-breakfast owners might get linked to the Web page of their state tourism office.

360 **Heed the four "Be's" of effective e-mail:**
- *Be conversational.* Write as you speak. Keep your messages casual and informal.
- *Be swift.* Respond instantly. All it takes is one click of the "reply" option.
- *Be colorful.* Vibrant words, humor, and CAPITALS always attract attention.

- *Be succinct.* Brief is best. Don't exceed 24 lines, or about one computer screen.
—Wally Bock, *Cyberpower Alert!* newsletter

361 **Let 'em know where you'll be—and when you'll be there.** Keep key people up to date on your schedule. Distribute personal calendars with the latest information on key projects and travel plans. Include phone numbers and addresses.

Let people know how and when you'll contact them.

362 **Keep current on your contacts.** Create a list of individuals you need to talk to at least monthly. Develop a computer file for each one, complete with data on previous conversations, future discussion topics, relevant news items, etc. Establish an agenda for each call. Evaluate each relationship periodically to determine its current and potential value to you.

363 **Discuss payoffs, not products.** Telephone sales expert Art Sobczak advises that you focus follow-up calls on customers' results rather than on your services. Ask how much their business has grown since they invested in your services.

364 **Use the first call to set up the next.** Close your first conversation with prospects with advice, suggestions, tips and ideas for them to work on. Follow up periodically to offer your encouragement and support.

Some good closing lines for an opening call, according to Sobczak:

- "I suggest..."
- "If I were in your situation, here's what I would do..."
- "My advice is to..."
- "Here's all we need to do to get started..."
- "It will be very simple to begin the process..."

365 **Provide quality in every call.** Remind your prospect of your previous conversation and share this call's agenda.

Deliver value by providing good news, useful information, worthwhile ideas, etc. Include industry information from which they could benefit, or details about your new special offer.

366 **Send a note.** Follow up a sales presentation with a handwritten note reinforcing one or two benefits of your service or products. Use the note to confirm a future meeting, or to suggest one.

367 **Follow your prospects' follow-up advice.** Ask them how they would like you to stay in touch. They may be more receptive once they're given the choice between your Web page, newsletters, e-mail and other options.

368 **Seek their help, get their business.** Don't invite a prospect to lunch to seek her business. Seek her advice, instead. The conver-

sation will surely turn to what you do— and how she would benefit from it.
—138 Quick Ideas To Get More Clients by Howard Shenson and Jerry Wilson

369 **If you seek input, provide outcomes.** Advise prospects of the results of the market research to which they contribute. Share your finds from a survey or questionnaire.

370 **Get feedback by fax or e-mail.** You'll receive better returns on your surveys when you use fax or e-mail rather than the phone or mail. Keep your questions short and easy, the kind for which "yes/no" and "agree/disagree" answers would be appropriate. Don't send anything unsolicited.

371 **Ask, "How did it go?"** A simple question—but a powerful one to pose to a new client the day after you provided a service or assisted in another way. The sooner you call, the more your client will appreciate it—and the easier it will be for you to correct and defuse a problem.

372 **Promote after the sale.** Promoting yourself *after* the sale or transaction creates a lasting impression. Jerry R. Wilson, in *Word of Mouth Marketing*, tells about the boat dealer who provides a cooler with beverages and hot dogs to new boat owners; and the travel agents who greet clients at the airport with a flight bag full of maps, coupons, suntan lotion, etc.

373 **Follow with a photo.** Carry a camera during a meeting with a prospect and client—and have a photo taken of the two of you. Then send a copy along with your thanks.

Take advantage of every photo op—ribbon cuttings, contract signings, ground breakings, etc.—to capture the two of you on film. Mat it, frame it—and your customer will keep it.

374 **Use vouchers to bring 'em back.** Send $20 reactivation vouchers to customers who haven't ordered for six months. Send "we miss you" cards along with vouchers to ex-clients who haven't recontacted you in more than a year.

Few will turn it down, and still fewer will spend only $20.
—Jerry Fisher in *Entrepreneur* magazine

375 **Assist your advocates.** Provide your "references" with suggested comments they can share about you. Supply them with remarks they can use about your credibility, accomplishments, personal traits, etc.
—*Career Power* by Richard Rinella and Claire Robbins

376 **Elicit testimonials on evaluation forms.** Give your customers an evaluation form that includes the question: "What did you like most about the service or product I provided?"

377 **Elicit success stories.** Ask questions like, "How did my product or service save you money?" (...save you time, ...improve your life, ...increase your business, etc.).

378 **Ask for testimonials at contract time.** Seek testimonials from customers when their contracts expire or at any other time they're considering whether to renew your service.

Your request will focus their attention on what makes you a valuable supplier. That could result in appreciative orders and referrals.
—*Seven Pillars of Sales Success* by Jonathan Evetts

379 **Get real.** Request several sheets of original letterhead from clients who agree to write you a testimonial letter. Ask them to create the letter on a blank sheet, so that you can reproduce it on their letterhead. Testimonials on a firm's letterhead, rather than on copies of it, come across as more authentic and professional.

380 **Request reasons.** Following a sale, ask your customer to jot down on back of his or her business card one or two reasons they did business with you. Insert the cards into a sheet of plastic sleeves that are available at office supply stores.
—*Superstar Sales Secrets* by Barry J. Farber

381 **Get a letter before they get away.** Request a testimonial or reference letter from a purchasing agent, buyer, or liaison *before* he or she leaves the company.

Act early—before personnel changes or promotions leave you empty-handed. Once your contact moves on, remain in touch. Ask for introductions—to the successor at the old company, and to sources at the new one.

If your sales manager or boss is about to move on, request a recommendation letter now. You may be unable to get one later.

382 **Tributes for testimonials.** Offer free products or gifts to those customers who write testimonial letters explaining how they profited and benefited from your products and services.

383 **Keep a breakdown on your buyers.** That means names, dates, quantities, and purchase order numbers. That will enable you to stay in touch with them—and prospective buyers to contact them for references.

384 **Get referrals when you get feedback.** Elicit referrals from those you work for by including on an evaluation the question: "Do you know of anyone else who would be interested in my services?"

385 **Stress the value of referrals.** Tell your clients that your business is based on them, that the majority of your business comes from them, and that you would appreciate any and all of their recommendations.
   —*Getting Business to Come to You* by Paul & Sarah Edwards and Laura Clampitt Douglas

386 **Tell 'em who you're looking for, and why.** Communicate clearly about your business, and the referrals you seek.

Help others help you by providing guidelines, such as "who among your suppliers might use my services?" or "of all of your contacts in your business and professionals group, who is most likely to need my products?"

387 **Offer cash for contacts.** Enclose money along with a thank-you note to someone who refers business to you. A finder's fee may appeal to those who wouldn't otherwise send business your way.

388 **Barter for promotional assistance.** If clients can't afford to pay the full price for your services, consider offering them a reduced rate in exchange for referrals, testimonials, introductory letters, free advertising space in their publications, etc.

389 **Ask for an introduction.** Ask your referral source to call ahead or write a letter of introduction for you. Sometimes they can do it while you're in their office!

390 **Let 'em know what you're up to.** Provide your referral sources with updated copies of your marketing materials. That will enlighten them about the direction your business is taking. The more information you provide, the more help they can supply.

391 **Join professional associations.** Get active in the professional organization(s) related to your field, and inform other members of your area of specialization. That's sure to lead to referrals.

392 **Ask your audience for referrals.** When you deliver a speech, distribute a form seeking feedback and information about others who could benefit from your services.

393 **Recontact the audience.** Following your speech, obtain a mailing list of attendees and follow up with a note describing your products and services.

394 **Talk local, go national.** If you deliver a speech to a local group, ask the director for a referral to the regional or national organization with which the group is affiliated. Also, seek an introduction to the editor of the trade publication for the national group.

395 **Renew old contacts.** Host an event for former clients and influential contacts with whom you've lost touch. Seek referrals, additional business, and promotional advice from them.

396 **Involve your staff in marketing.** Appoint each employee to your personal marketing staff. Provide them with business cards, brochures, and other promotional materials they can distribute on your behalf.

397 **Widen your referral source network.** Anyone who does business *with* you should receive marketing materials *from* you. That goes for vendors, suppliers, accountants, bankers—anyone who serves you in any way. Let them know you would appreciate their help in distributing materials to promising prospects.

Chances are the suppliers and others, eager to retain your business, will assist you in any way they can.

398 **Keep in touch with allied professionals.** Develop relationships with companies in related fields with whom you can share promotional efforts.

If you want to align with other professionals, contact them regularly. Include the names of your "allies" in your databases and on your mailing lists.

399 **Recall their interest, not objections.** When calling back individuals who weren't ready to do business with you earlier, remind them of their earlier interest, rather than their earlier objections.

Instead of recalling their previous budget concerns, remind them of their initial interest in your products and services.

400 **Go until "no."** Pursue promising prospects until they tell you they're not interested.

Set a reasonable time limit for your pursuit, but don't assume that an unreturned phone call indicates disinterest. Even the hottest of prospects may be too busy to answer your messages.

Try several methods to reach them and, if you finally do, greet them with genuine enthusiasm.

CHAPTER NINE

Dare to Be Different

"Anybody who is any good is different from anybody else."
—the late Supreme Court Justice Felix Frankfurter

I vividly remember awakening to the sounds of the milk truck grinding up the driveway. Then...the screech of the brakes, the squeak of a sliding door, and the clink of milk bottles. Finally, the footsteps as Jerry—the milk-man from Sun Valley Dairy—approached our back door to drop off the milk.

As Jerry would open the door to deposit the bottles and pick up the empties, he would lean in and say something like: "Good morning! It's partly cloudy and cool this morning, with a 20-mile-an-hour wind from the West. But better bring an umbrella this afternoon. There's a 70 percent chance of rain."

The daily ritual both fascinated and perplexed me. One wintry morning, I slipped on a pair of galoshes and trailed Jerry out the door onto the driveway.

"Say, Jerry." I called out to the retreating figure on the snowy driveway. "Why do you do that? Why do you give us the weather forecast every day?"

Jerry stopped, glanced over his left shoulder, and broke into a smile.

"Kid, I do it for one reason," he said. "I do it because the other guys don't."

I didn't get it at the time—I was, after all, only seven. But I get it now. Jerry had given me my first lesson in "dare to be different" self-promotion.

* * * * *

Why you?

That's the question in the back of the minds of all those you seek to influence, impress, or do business with.

At a time when so many businesses are vying for their attention, why should they listen to you? At a time when they're bombarded with so many sales messages— 1,200 a day from print and broadcast media alone— why should they care about yours?

What makes *you* different?

I hope you've given some serious thought to this question that was raised in Chapter 3—and that you'll continue to do so. You can't make the personal sale until you can differentiate yourself. You won't be remembered until you set yourself apart from your competitors.

> "In order to be irreplaceable, one must always be different."
> —Coco Chanel

George Washington Carver, the noted agricultural chemist and educator, put it this way: "When you do the common things in life in an uncommon way, you will command the attention of the world."

You can make the greatest impact on those you seek to influence only when you promote your unique message in unique ways.

"I don't care what you do," campaign strategist James Carville once advised presidential candidate Bill Clinton. "But just make damn sure it's big and different."

When it comes to marketing yourself, there are really only two choices. You can do as your competitors do—or you can do it differently.

Should you duplicate the marketing strategies of your competitors, you choose to play the self-promotion "Same Game" referred to earlier.

They Dared to Be Different

Earl Nightengale, one of the most successful radio commentators in history, chose not to play the Same Game after he got his first announcing job at KTAR in Phoenix.

His goal was to elevate himself to a bigger and better announcing job at the network level. His fellow KTAR broadcasters teased him about his attempts to promote himself to a network job.

Nightengale later recalled how he gave "so much pizzazz to the local commercials— whether for the local mortuary or sporting goods store—that my announcer friends soon dubbed me 'network' and kidded me and found my efforts ludicrous."

When Nightengale announced his plans in 1949 to buy a one-way ticket to Chicago to seek employment with network radio, the other announcers responded with "unbelieving stares and vociferous arguments" about why his efforts would fail.

But his skills and his self-promotion efforts paid off. In Chicago, CBS-affiliate WBBM offered him a network contract that, he said, included "more money than I had dreamed of earning."

By daring to be different, and choosing not to join in the Same Game, Nightengale found the kind of success and security that would elude most of his former colleagues.

The alternative to the Same Game is to sell yourself in a different way. It's a more challenging option, requiring that you map your own course and clear your own path. It requires creativity, imagination, and persistence. It's a lot of work—but, if you're serious about self-promotion, it's the only way to go.

Wayne Dyer, the psychologist and author, decided that being different was the only way for *him* to go in the mid-1970s. Having failed to convince national talk shows to book him to discuss his new book, *Your Erroneous Zones,* he loaded his car with hundreds of copies.

For a year, he traveled to small towns across America, appearing on any radio or TV talk show that would have him.

On the air, Dyer would mention the phone numbers of local bookstores that, he said, carried his books. Following the interviews, he would drive over to the bookstores and introduce himself.

Store owners would tell him they had received calls for his book. Dyer sold the stores cases of the books— and he signed them on-site.

Before long, Dyer was invited to appear on *The Tonight Show*, and *Your Erroneous Zones* became one of the best-selling nonfiction books of the decade.

Why Show Your Uniqueness?

Why should *you* go to the extra effort of selling yourself differently? Why concern yourself with doing your own marketing thing, when it's so much easier to follow the lead of others?

> "Every style that is not boring is good."
> —Voltaire

You Owe It to Yourself

You're a unique, special, one-of-a kind individual. There's no one else exactly like you. You're an original.

Talk about yourself in ways that others talk about themselves—or fail to talk about yourself at all—and you hide your uniqueness and special talents. You sell yourself short. You miss out on opportunities, fail to get what's coming to you, and fall short of your potential.

When it comes to achieving your professional goals, your time is short. You should give self-promotion your best effort today, for you may not get the chance tomorrow.

"There is no dress rehearsal," Mahatma Gandhi, the great Hindu nationalist and spiritual leader once said. "This is the day."

You Owe It to Others

Your responsibility to your customers is to offer them the best possible service. One way to do that is to offer them options.

By promoting your differences, you make available options that customers won't be able to find elsewhere. You educate customers and make it easier for them to distinguish between you and your competitors.

Today's customers *expect* options. They're accustomed to entertainment complexes with dozens of theaters, TV sets with hundreds of channels, video rental stores with thousands of titles.

To get new and repeat business, you need to educate your prospects and customers on the many ways that you're different, and on the many product and service options that you offer.

Take It from Walt Disney

"To be successful in business, you must be unique," he said. "You must be so different that if people want what you have, they must come to you to get it."

—Walt Disney

You Can't Win the Game by Being the Same

Victory on the job as well as on the playing field comes to those who make the greatest effort to outdo the competition. Make that effort to distinguish yourself and you'll be a winner.

Merely copy the efforts of your competitors, and you'll be a "wannabe." You'll never get ahead.

Perceptions May Be a Problem

What do people think about when they think about you?

Many salespeople readily admit that their prospects associate words like "slick," "pushy," and "dishonest" with their profession.

Jeff Thull, a professional speaker and author, says that "most people see salesmen as vultures sitting on telephone wires, waiting for a squirrel to get hit. That would be a buying signal."

As a self-promoter, you're in the sales business—the personal sales business—so you must deal with that kind of baggage. The best way to confront negative perceptions is to differentiate yourself and market yourself in unique ways.

The message you must convey to the skeptics: "I understand how you feel about those in my profession. But you need to understand that I'm different."

Start Your Engines

How do your launch this unique self-marketing campaign?

Begin by appreciating the "you" that you're about to promote. List ten ways you differ from your competitors. Jot down your top five "onlys." Compile ten benefits that you alone offer. Do all that, and you'll soon be able to talk about yourself as skillfully as you talk about your products and services. That will *really* distinguish you.

Some other suggestions:

- Stop, look and listen. Observe what your competitors are doing to market themselves, and resolve to promote *yourself* differently.
- Take responsibility. Make your own breaks. Let others bellyache about bad luck, or a poor sales territory, or their health, or the weather. Rather than play the "Blame Game," look into the mirror and say: "What is to be is up to me."
- Sell your "onlys." By now (I hope) you've figured out what "onlys" you offer. Consider your experience, the awards and recognition you've received, the clients you serve, your area of specialization, your staff, your unique talents. Okay, now spread the word.
- Reach out to prospects in ways that surprise them (see Chapter 7 for ideas).
- Follow up with prospects and clients in ways that surprise them (see Chapter 8).
- Make a splash. Stir things up by making predictions, analyzing trends, issuing warnings—and including them in letters to the editors of key publications.
- Walk on the (personal promotion) wild side.

Some "Wildsiders"

Meet **David Alan Miller**, conductor of the Albany Symphony Orchestra. He shows up at his job riding an elephant one day, then dresses like Batman or Mozart the next. His philosophy: "Standing there in a dark suit simply isn't enough anymore."

Or take **Sid Friedman**, a Philadelphia insurance agent. He learns a CEO he's been trying to reach is flying to Chicago. Friedman books himself next to his prospect's first-class seat, sells him a million-dollar policy by the time they land, turns around and flies home.

And **Barbara Notarius**, a bed-and-breakfast inn owner in Croton-on-Hudson, New York. She writes an article on "The Ten Best Places to Kiss in New York"— and includes her inn on the list. The honeymoon suite's been booked ever since.

And **Thomas Burke**, a commodity trader. He reports to work at the Chicago Board of Trade's "pits" wearing magenta, lime-green, or silver lamé jackets. "I'd come in buck naked if I could," he says. "As it is, the more obnoxious the jacket, the better. The louder it is, the more I can rest my voice and let my jacket draw the attention."

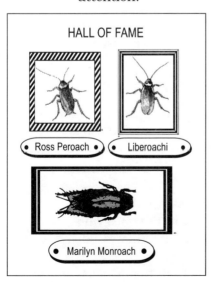

HALL OF FAME

Ross Peroach   Liberoachi

Marilyn Monroach

And **Michael Bohdan**, a Texas pest control professional. He transforms his insect collection into "The Cockroach Hall of Fame." Gives the critters names like Marilyn Monroach, Ross Peroach, and Liberoachi. He lands on TV nearly 500 times.

And **Bob Brachman**. Rejected in his attempts to date a woman named Arlene, he runs ads on billboards near her Milwaukee office with sayings like "Swellsy, Dandy, Peachy Keen, Why, Oh, Why, Are You So Mean?" The billboard courtship gets international publicity; eventually she relents, and ultimately they marry.

And those other marketing mavericks out there sending thank-you notes by carrier pigeon, or wearing costumes and getting in front of the *Today Show's* live outdoor cameras, or delivering sales presentations in crowded elevators, or decorating their showrooms and offices in bizarre ways.

Lindsey Nelson's Mission

Those who take the walk on the marketing wild side are on a mission, of course. The mission: personal promotion. The motive: to attract attention. The methods: whatever it takes.

Lindsey Nelson embarked on his mission as the radio announcer for the New York Mets in 1962, their first and worst season. The team was to lose 120 games that year, prompting manager Casey Stengel at one point to inquire: "Can't anybody here play this game?"

Not many could, and Nelson sought a way to attract public attention to the pathetic team—and, more importantly, network attention to himself. He began to show up at games in psychedelic sport coats, hardly standard wearing apparel for broadcasters of that era. The gaudy jackets—of which Nelson eventually owned 700—became legendary, and so did Lindsey Nelson, even though he was the voice of one of the worst baseball teams in history.

The Risk

Perhaps you think you're not ready for a walk on the wild side, that "daring to be different" in the way you market your services seems risky.

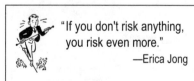

"If you don't risk anything, you risk even more."
—Erica Jong

Consider this. The only ones at risk are those who fail to promote themselves at all. They're the ones who underestimate their value, and who think they're not *worth* promoting.

Through that oversight, they risk their financial security. They may end up accepting salaries that are too low, undervaluing their services, and lowering their prices.

Show me someone who regularly cuts his prices or lowers her fees, and I'll show you someone who wastes time and energy. If only they could rechannel some of that price-cutting energy into setting themselves apart and promoting themselves differently, money wouldn't be an issue.

But, for far too many professionals, money is and always has been an issue. A study by the Vass Company, an Atlanta sales training firm, indicated that over a 15-year period, 90 percent of salespeople offered to lower their price before they were asked to do so. *Sales and Marketing Management* magazine reports that 80 percent of salespeople fail to close the deal when their customers are ready to buy.

Something's missing from these pictures: self-confidence. Clearly, many sales professionals don't believe in who they are, let alone what they sell. They attach too little importance to themselves, and too much to price.

The fact is, you can set and get greater fees, always obtain "your" price, and dramatically increase your income once you sufficiently differentiate yourself from those who charge less.

Your price is not the primary concern of your prospects and clients.

First and foremost, they are looking for the best solutions to their problems. Distinguish yourself from your competitors, many of whom focus on price, by coming up with the best solutions—then your success is assured.

> "In whatever you do...make sure there is a 'wow factor'—something that will grab people's attention and make them notice that you've sweated the details."
> —Carl Sewell,
> *Customers for Life*

Unique Service

One of the best ways to set yourself apart from price-focused competitors is to offer outstanding service.

Customer service training is a staple for many organi-

Cut Prices, Cut Profits

For years, a group of interior designers in Omaha confronted severe price competition, and were quick to blame the Nebraska Furniture Mart for it.

The Mart, with showroom space exceeding that of several football fields, is the largest privately-owned facility of its kind in the United States. It sells everything from futons to fabrics at prices well below those that local designers would charge if they bought the items wholesale and sold them to customers.

Some local designers became so concerned about the Mart that they resolved to cut their fees in order to hang onto customers. As much as they groused about the idea of a "price war," they mounted one. Fee cutting became the rule rather than the exception.

These designers spent so much time and energy futzing with their fees that they became experts on price warfare. Many could tell you more about price undercutting than they could about themselves. They knew more about discounting than they did about self-promotion.

None of them could easily list services or benefits that they alone offered. None could easily explain why prospects should work with them rather than shopping through the Mart or discount catalogs.

None could spell out what made them different.

If only they'd converted all that price war energy into self-promotion. If only they'd created marketing messages defining their differences, and listing the benefits that they offered but the Mart didn't—or couldn't. If only they"d promoted the value of their service and their expertise.

If only they had dared to be different from the Mart in the ways they promoted themselves, there wouldn't have been a price war.

But they didn't. And there was.

---

zations today. Dare to be different by exceeding the ordinary skills your competitors learn, and offering *extraordinary* service.

Wal-Mart knows a thing or two about doing that something "extra."

Walk into a Wal-Mart store, and a greeter gives you a cart, along with a warm "hello." It's a nice gesture—and it's also good business. Wal-Mart surveyed their customers and discovered that shoppers purchase over 10 percent more when they push a cart.

Do you make it easier for your customers to buy from you? Do you fill out purchase orders and other paperwork for them? Do you inform them of all the ways you can help them by providing a complete list of your products and services? Do you offer a toll-free number and fax-on-demand information sheets and updates?

Dare to be different by providing extraordinary follow-up. That means contacting buyers within a few days after delivering your products, and inquiring if those items met their needs and expectations. It means calling them later to find out how everything is working, and providing them with an evaluation form.

It means sending personal notes, e-mail messages, newsletters, faxes, and other materials to show your continuing interest in their well-being. And it means offering free training and consultation on how they can make the most of their purchases.

Why Try for 100% Perfection?

Why "dare to be different" and attempt to provide 100 percent customer service? Why not be satisfied with less than that?

Read on...

If 99.9 percent is good enough, then...

- Two million documents will be lost by the IRS this year.
- 22,000 checks will be deducted from the wrong bank accounts in the next 60 minutes.
- 1,314 phone calls will be misplaced by telecommunication services every minute.
- 12 babies will be given to the wrong parents each day.
- 18,322 pieces of mail will be mishandled in the next hour.
- 880,000 credit cards will contain misinformation.
- $9,690 will be spent today and every day in the future on defective, unsafe sporting equipment.
- 268,500 defective tires will be shipped this year.
- 20,000 incorrect drug prescriptions will be written in the next 12 months.
- 107 incorrect medical procedures will be performed by the end of the day today.

—Insight, Syncrude Canada Ltd.,
Communications Division

It's Easy to Stand Out

You'll stand out from your competitors if you're available—any time, all the time. Successful self-promoters are accessible via office phone, cellular phone, digital pager, voice mail, and every other technological means. And they return all messages promptly.

Once you do make contact with prospects, welcome rather than avoid their objections, even if they insist that your price is too high, or that they are fully satisfied with their current suppliers.

Ask the right questions. Offer unique guarantees. And, throughout the process, talk their talk and express yourself in their language rather than your own. Avoid "salespeak."

The payoff to you of offering superior customer service is that you will stand out from competitors who offer less. You will come across not as a salesperson, but as a "buyer facilitator."

You will be able to establish long-term relationships with clients, rather than having to rely on single sales.

Surprise Your Customers

You'll make the personal sale if you "wow" those you serve.

Surprise your customers with something they don't expect, and you will stand out in their minds.

Phil Romano, founder of the national hamburger chain called Fuddruckers, skillfully used this element of surprise when he ran a small restaurant called Macaroni's. Randomly-selected customers who dined there received an invitation to return and eat free on a future Monday or Tuesday night.

The result: Macaroni's was packed wall-to-wall on nights when other restaurants in town struggled to remain open.

What's in a Name?

If you're starting a new business, use a little creative thinking in deciding on your company name. That's what an Orlando, Florida. auto body shop did when it came up with the name "Wreck-a-Mended."

Then there was "Substitoothes," a temporary-employment agency for dental hygienists in El Sobrante, California. And "Low Dough Tow," a Sacramento, California towing firm. And "Latte Dah," a St. Paul, Minnesota espresso cart.

Last but not least: "Go to Your Room," a Seattle furniture outlet, and "Counter Fitters," a Canadian kitchen and bath dealer.

The gimmick cost Macaroni's a bit—but Romano more than made up for it with additional business generated from enthusiastic word-of-mouth referrals.

You can make a big impact simply by doing little things differently.

Take the sales rep for a medical equipment company whose sales have soared since he began bringing in bagels for the receptionists and nurses.

And the area director for a multilevel marketing company who sends out microwave popcorn along with his promotional videos.

And the insurance salesman who distributes humorous holiday cards on unusual holidays, like Tax Freedom Day.

Dare Yourself

How you decide to promote yourself is less important than that you do it in ways that your competitors do not.

Dare yourself to be different.

Dare to be different in the words you choose to describe who you are and what you do.

Dare to be different in the methods by which you promote yourself.

Dare to be different in the niche you create, and the market you pursue.

Dare to discover the difference that *being* different in your promotion can make.

Action Ideas and Tips

401 **Use your imagination.** It's your most valuable personal promotion resource.

Think out of the box and let your thoughts run free. Seriously consider marketing ideas that your competitors don't even dream about.

402 **Adopt a look that's unorthodox for your profession.** Dress up—or down—to stand out. Wear a flamboyant hat, funky glasses, wild ties or scarves, shoes that don't match, glow-in-the-dark colors—anything that will set you apart from your competitors.

403 **Use a nickname as a personal marketing tool.** Choose a name that identifies your expertise and add it to your marketing materials. Are you "Mr. Marketing" or the "Corporate Mergermeister" or the "Technology Wizard"?

404 **Have a day declared in your honor.** Do something good for the community, state or nation, and you can get a "day" set aside for you. Share news of your good deed with members of the city council, the state senate and the state house of representatives, the mayor, and the governor. Request a citation and a proclamation of a day in your honor.

Examples of good deeds that may qualify you for this recognition:

- long service to a local civic organization
- participation in a local fund drive
- assistance in getting a law or resolution passed
- efforts in local charitable causes
- activities to beautify your town or improve its quality of life

—*The Unabashed Self-Promoter's Guide* by Jeffrey Lant

405 **Add a gimmick to your marketing materials.** It can be an odd-shaped product sample, a talking business card or other comical cards, a magnetic brochure, a sticker, a badge, a pin—anything that will make your materials more memorable. Whatever you select should be offbeat, and should bear your name.

406 **Put some fun in your photo.** Come up with a promotional picture that will be remembered in ways that photos of your competitors are not.

Steer clear of the standard "head shot" or professional pose. Create a photo showing you in an unusual setting, doing something unusual, or wearing something unusual.

407 **Offer an outrageous "frequent buyer" award.** "Outrageous," as in an around-the-world trip, a mink coat, or a fancy sports car. Make the award available to your "dream client"—anyone who purchases such a large amount of your products and services that your lifetime prosperity is assured.

What you won't get, of course, is a winner. What you *will* get, through proper promotion, is plenty of free publicity.

408 **Hold a "what you like most about me" contest.** Encourage customers to submit 250-words-or-less entries spelling out what they consider to be the most important benefits you provide. Offer a prize for the winners, and reprint their letters in your marketing materials.

The exercise will reinforce customer loyalty—and provide you with some powerful new testimonial letters.

409 **Sponsor another offbeat contest.**

Invite media representatives to judge it, and hold a news conference to announce it.

For a commercial office designer, "offbeat" could be a messiest office contest. For a clothing retailer, it could be an ugliest jacket contest. For a restaurant owner, it could be a pasta eating contest. For a pest control professional, it could be a largest spider contest.

410 **Hit a home run with a hole in one.** Offer a big prize— perhaps $10,000—at a local tournament for any golfer who gets a hole in one on the ninth hole. Donate half the money to a local charity.

Notify the media—and be available, along with an enlarged display of your logo—at the hole. The TV cameras are sure to be on hand.

Offer a big prize to a local tournament for: a 300-game in bowling; , a no-hitter in softball, or a score of one million points in Pac-Man .

—Streetfighting by Jeff Slutsky

411 **Speak out.** Take a controversial stand, make an unusual prediction, discuss a shocking trend, issue a warning, sponsor an outrageous event—and hold a news conference to announce it. What you say, and how and when you say it, can draw media attention, even if you're not a public figure.

412 **Face off against a foe.** Identify the leading critics of your industry—and offer to debate them on the air. Contact a local broadcast outlet about running the debate.

Or, try contacting the leading trade publications in your field about running "point-counterpoint" editorials or articles by you and your adversaries.

413 **Go against the flow.** Challenge conventional wisdom in your industry and deliberately do what the others don't. Be a contrarian—and promote the fact.

If your competitors cut their fees, raise yours. If others advertise in the Yellow Pages, avoid doing so. If the trend is toward specializing, offer more general services. Determine the consensus in your field, and promote alternative views.

414 Offer your help to a public figure. Launch a media blitz in which you offer your services for free to the president, governor, mayor, a local professional athlete, or other big names in the news to improve his or her job performance. Use a media release, letter to the editor, or even a news conference to identify the problem ("Governor X can't balance the state budget"), and offer your assistance ("I'll donate two weeks of my time to review his books").

415 Don't use ordinary means to announce extraordinary developments. You're *expected* to send out cards to inform others about your business. Why not do the *unexpected?* Send out a birth announcement when you launch a new product or service. Mail anniversary cards to celebrate another year in business. Distribute engagement notices when you take on a partner, or merge with another firm.

416 Recognize the "other" holidays. Limit your holiday card-giving to events like April Fool's Day, Ground Hog Day, the Summer Solstice, etc. Choose dates that are appropriate for your profession. A landscaper, for example, could distribute cards on Arbor Day.

417 Promote yourself on offbeat days, in offbeat ways. Use *Chase's Annual Events* as a source for unusual dates and events on which to publicize yourself. Consider timing your promotion to coincide with unconventional events like "Lumpy Rug Day,"
"National Bathroom Reading Week," the World Cow Chip Throwing Championship, etc.

418 Create a celebration. Think of your own offbeat cause or event that you want the world to celebrate. Contact *Chase's* (312-540-4500) about including it, and your name, in their directory.

If your name is Roger, how about proposing "National Roger Week?" If you're a stockbroker, you might introduce "Take a Stockbroker to Lunch Day."

The possibilities are endless. The only criteria is that they attract attention to you, the founder.

419 Leave a message with a message. Write yours on a telephone message pad sheet, and enlarge it to standard paper size. Then fax it to the individual you attempted to reach.

That's not the way professionals are used to getting their messages. It will make a hit.

420 Take it to the top. Promote yourself with a sign or logo printed on the tops of your company vehicles. It's a great way to gain the attention of people who work in office buildings.

421 Publicize your clients and yourself. Write articles about how clients benefit from your services. They'll appreciate the free publicity—and you'll appreciate the additional business it will generate.

422 **Make yourself a star.** Write an article on the fastest-rising local stars in your industry, and include yourself in it. Use a pseudonym in the by-line—and in pitching the story to the local media. Or, have an associate contact the media for you.

423 **"Play cards" with prospects.** Request several business cards from each prospect. Explain that you want to keep one and pass the others on to business associates. It's a good way to "flatter and impress" your prospects.

—*How Good Guys Grow Rich* by Adriane G. Berg and Milton Gralla

424 **Call for the secretary rather than the boss.**

Everyone wants to talk to the decision maker. The problem is, gatekeepers often get in the way.

Get the receptionists, executive assistants, and office managers on your side by forming relationships with them. Ask the kind of questions, show the kind of interest, and follow up with the kind of notes that others do not. That may motivate them to open the gate to the person in charge.

425 **Call when it's least expected.** Check in at unusual times and places. Call prospects early in the morning or late at night—or on holidays those prospects don't celebrate.

Offer to accompany them on the errands, if that's the only time they can spare.

426 **Don't sound like a salesperson.** Sales expert Tom

Hopkins recommends the following word substitutions:

Instead of...	Use...
price	total investment
down payment	initial investment
monthly payment	monthly investment
contract	paperwork
buy	own
sign	authorize, OK, approve
deal	opportunity
appointment	visit
objections	areas of concern
sell	get you involved

427 **Focus on what to ask, not what to say.** Let your competitors spend their prep time rehearsing their facts. Spend yours on rehearsing your questions.

Work on presenting the right questions in the right way. Perfect your wording, timing and inflection. Your information won't mean much if it doesn't relate to your prospects' needs and wants. It's important to talk your talk—about your products and services. But you'll stand out if you're able to talk *their* talk.

428 **Prepare for "the questions from Hell."** Ponder the questions which *aren't* likely to surface—but which would be killers if they did.

Consider the questions you don't want to hear: the unreasonable, irrelevant, biased, make-you-sweat kind that could only come up in the worst of circumstances.

Prepare for the worst. Before the meeting, have your staff pepper you with these worst-case-scenario questions. That will prevent you from being surprised and caught off guard later.

429 **Ask open-ended questions.** "Which of my services do you think will help you the most?" That's the kind of question to ask after contacting a prospect. Avoid questions that can be answered with a simple "yes" or "no."

Wrong: "Are you interested in any of my programs?"

Right: "Which of my programs do you find most interesting?"

Too often, prospects will tell you they haven't yet reviewed your materials. Find out when (time, day and date) they will, and make an appointment to talk then.

430 **Buy stock in a hot prospect.** Owning a single share entitles you to attend stockholder meetings, and receive annual reports and other inside information.

Go a step further, and become a shareholder in a *competitor's* company. That will educate you on how the other company is doing—and why.

431 **Make your ads odd.** Oddities in advertising attract attention. That's why, for example, the model in the Hathaway Shirt ads wore an eye patch.

To make your ads stand out:
- Vary their shape, sizes and colors—but avoid "props" that divert attention.
- Make the layouts "busy" rather than neat.
- Use photos rather than illustrations.

- Include before-and-after photos, if possible.

—*Direct Response*

432 **Offer guarantees that your competitors don't.** Consider using lifetime, "for as long as you own it" guarantees.

Promise to pick up unsatisfactory equipment at your expense. Offer loaners and replacements. Take care of all shipping and handling costs. Guarantee telephone support, or follow-up training. Those guarantees distinguish your products, your services and yourself.

433 **Make contact by cassette.** Send a cassette in a plain white envelope with a handwritten address, no return address, and a "personal" mark on the front. On the tape, identify yourself, note that your comments will be brief, and then relay a concise and benefit-oriented message. Include the time and date when you will follow up with a call.

—*Can I Have Five Minutes of Your Time?* by Hal Becker

434 **Refute the "current vendor" argument.** A prospect expresses satisfaction with the supplier they're now using. End of conversation? Dare to be different by pursuing the prospect further. Advise them of the wisdom of putting some eggs in *your* basket.

Note that, in this era of mergers, acquisitions, and buyouts, no organization's future is guaranteed. Suggest that the prospect consider you as a secondary supplier—just in case.

435 **Welcome objections.** Think of objections—about price, selection, delivery, etc.—as buying signals. If there's no objection, there may be no deal. Studies show that sales calls with customer objections end successfully nearly two thirds of the time—far greater than when no objections come up.

Generally, people won't take the time to argue against your ideas if they're not at least somewhat interested in them—and you.

436 **Answer price questions with more questions.** Don't become defensive about price objections. Turn the issue into an advantage by asking questions like:

- What are you comparing our price to?
- Can you afford not to take advantage of the benefits that only we offer?
- Do you know how we're different?
- Do you know how we'll actually save you money in the long run?
- What would it be worth it to you to make a change?
- What would it cost you if you didn't?

437 **Reach for the Rule of Three.** When you're at an impasse on price with a prospect, don't give up—or give in—without using this response developed by sales trainer Tom Hopkins:

"Customers look for three things: the finest quality, the best service, and the lowest investment. No company can offer all three. Which of the three would you be most willing to give up? Fine quality? Excellent service? Or the lowest fee?"

Usually, customers say that they would pay more if that would assure better quality and service.

438 **Share what might have been.** Don't give up when a prospect won't return your call. Send a note spelling out in print the benefits you would have described in person. Seeing the information in writing might motivate the prospect to contact you.

439 **Accept bad news in a good way.** You'll be remembered in ways that your competitors aren't if you send a personal note after your proposal is rejected. Thank the prospect for considering you and express interest in serving them in the future.

440 **Require referrals.** Don't leave referrals and testimonials to chance. Include them in the terms of your contract, along with a "due date" to assure a quick response.

441 **Accentuate the negative.** Make your promotional materials stand out by stating reasons why prospects should *not* use your services.

Your "Reasons Not to Hire Me" list should, of course, be outrageous, and include reasons like "if you prefer wasting money on higher-priced competitors," "if you don't care about outstanding customer service, " and "If lifetime guarantees mean nothing to you."

442 **Get their help when you get their business.** Don't wait until you have a "history" with new clients to seek their assistance. Act immediately to recruit them as references. Ask them to connect you with their other offices and with their vendors and suppliers, introduce you to additional prospects; consider you for future projects, etc.

443 **Get their upgrade when you get their business.** Presell brand new clients on extended and additional services. Use the initial "grace period" to suggest next steps for your relationship, sell equipment upgrades, contract for follow-up service, etc.

444 **Tape your testimonials.** Create video testimonials by having an assistant interview your clients about how they benefit from your services. Show the video to prospects and others you seek to influence.

445 **Make your name live on.** Use words and images to assure your name gets remembered. I tell people my name is "Berns"—as in "first degree" or "side," but with an "e" instead of a "u." Someone named "Hammer" could refer to the tool, while a "Graham" could mention the cracker.

A Sherlock Holmes cap might help an individual named Holmes be remembered, while a bow-and-arrow pin could do the job for a woman named "Archer."

446 **When a competitor quits business, build yours.** Buy your competitor's old phone number and install a new line. Advise callers of the change, and of your availability to serve their needs.

447 **Get a Sugar Daddy.** Ask an organization seeking to reach your market to sponsor you.

Seek their financial support in return for sharing their message, distributing their information, and displaying their products. Offer to promote them in your sales and marketing materials.

448 **Don't play with your price.** Let competitors compromise *their* integrity by giving in to price pressure.

Reduce your price only when you reduce your service.

Advise those who bellyache over bucks that the fee provides them *you* as well as your products. Explain what differentiates you from competitors who charge less.

449 **Talk to strangers.** Engage anyone and everyone in conversation about their needs and your business. You've got nothing to lose— and income to gain. Step out of your comfort zone each time you step out of your office, and become a walking commercial and ambassador for your business. Stand out from competitors by being the most extroverted professional in your field.

450 **Underpromise; overdeliver.**

Quick Fixes

"Time is on my side, yes it is."
—The Rolling Stones

"I just don't have the *time* to market myself."
Sound familiar? It should. It's the most common excuse, along with lack of money, that professionals give for not promoting themselves more actively.

Perhaps you've used that excuse yourself, complaining that there "just aren't enough hours in the day" to get the word out about yourself.

You Have Time

But you *do* have the time. You have the time to network. You have the time to talk about yourself and your organization. You have the time to distribute personal promotion materials.

You have the time—provided you know how to use it.

Don't assume that personal marketing requires a commitment of great blocks of time.

Do you equate self-promotion with elaborate public relations and media campaigns, or national speaking tours, or Internet projects? Or complex strategies that require months of arduous research, and may or may not result in long-term payoffs?

Do you think you lack the time to sell yourself because making the personal sale *requires* a lot of extra time? The good news is that time isn't crucial.

Making your personal sale need not be a big deal.

In fact, it can be a series of little deals—minor moves you can make to set yourself apart from competitors.

There are several steps you can take—this month, this week, today!—to use your time better and gain quick results. Many of those steps don't require an extra effort on your part.

Consider how easy it is to piggyback the five-minute maneuvers listed on this page onto other activities.

The next time you talk to a former client, for example, ask for a referral or a testimonial letter. The next time you check in with a customer, ask him to write a letter of introduction for you. The next time you fulfill a customer's order, include a little gift in the box.

Clearly, there is no shortage of quick-fix self-promotion options. Base your selection on what it is you want to fix and what you like to do.

The first step is to zero in on your problem. Are you not reaching the right people? Are you not communicating with your customers? Are you failing to convert single sales into long-term relationships? Are there doubts about your credibility?

Pinpoint your number one marketing problem so that you can determine which of the quick fixes will work best for you.

Five-Minute Maneuvers

In 5 minutes or less, you can...

- Jot down your key achievements for the day and month
- List your five major marketing priorities for this month
- Create a five-question customer satisfaction survey
- Change your voice mail
- Ask a client for a referral and testimonial letter
- Ask a client for additional business
- Contact a prospect
- Contact a former client
- Share three ways that you differ from your competitors
- Meet five people at a networking event
- Distribute 10 business cards at a trade show
- Fax out three sets of personal promotional materials
- Send a note or e-mail message to a client or prospect
- Add a "P.S." to your direct mail
- Pitch a story idea about your company to a reporter
- Write a letter to the editor
- Send out an article reprint to three top prospects
- Have a top quality photo taken
- Get on the mailing list of top prospects & competitors
- Give something away
- Invite a decision maker to lunch

Gradually you'll develop your *own* short-cut strategies, as you get in the habit of using short-term solutions to tackle long-term marketing challenges.

Market Smarter, Not Harder

Given more time, would you promote yourself more effectively? Not necessarily. The personal sale takes some time, but, more importantly, it takes initiative, enthusiasm, and dedication.

No, you don't have to spend *more* time marketing yourself in order to make the personal sale. But you do have to make better use of your time.

One way to do that is to manage your time more effectively. Automating your sales correspondence can help. So can scheduling meetings over breakfast. So can keeping a separate list of Internet sites that you visit most often (bookmarking).

Mark Sanborn believes the best way to maximize your time is to create a list of your "10 MVP activities: the ones that are most valuable and profitable."

Sanborn, a Denver-based business educator, speaker, and author, recommends that you devote up to 80 percent of your day to those MVP activities because they provide the largest return on your investment of time and energy.

Minimize or eliminate nonrevenue-generating tasks, he says, and replace them with selling, upselling, cross-selling, or prospecting. That way "maintenance or operational activities" won't get in the way of making money.

Timing Counts

Another way to manage your time better is to work on your timing.

Ask the prospect on the

other end of the phone to call up your Web page while you're talking. Or fax her promotional material during the call. That's good timing.

Promote your service to a company a month before it begins planning its budget for the coming year. That's good timing.

Call a CEO at 7:30 a.m., before his secretary arrives to screen his calls. Or place the call at 6:45 p.m., after the secretary has departed. That's good timing.

Finish your personal presentation to the board *before* distributing supporting materials, so as not to divert attention from your message. That's good timing, too.

> "Time passes at a predetermined rate no matter what we do. It is a question not of managing the clock but of managing ourselves in respect to the clock...the heart of time management is management of self."
> —Alec Mackenzie, *The Time Trap: Managing Your Way Out*

Believe in Yourself

Capitalize on your personal promotion time by communicating an upbeat message about yourself, presenting yourself in a positive manner, and carrying yourself in a dignified way. It helps to adopt an upbeat outlook about self-marketing: that personal promotion is worth doing, and that you're worth promoting.

You can promote yourself more effectively by making some minor adjustments in the way you talk, the way you walk and the way you think—about yourself and about self-promotion.

Your attitude means everything to your self-promotion success. What you think and feel on the inside is worth a lot more than the tasks you perform on the outside.

Present Yourself to Your Public

If you're looking for better results in your business, present yourself in more positive ways. Some quick fixes can help you accomplish that.

The first of these is worth a million dollars, though it costs you nothing: smiling. You can't help but enhance your image by putting a warm, genuine smile on your face. "Genuine" as in authentic and sincere, rather than fake and forced.

In his book *How to Win Friends and Influence People,* Dale Carnegie included smiling in his list of the six best ways to get people to like you. But he emphasized that your smile must be the real thing.

"An insincere grin? No. That doesn't fool anybody. We know it is mechanical and we resent it," he wrote. "I am talking about a real smile, a heartwarming smile, a smile that comes from within, the kind of smile that will bring a good price in the marketplace."

> "A man without a smiling face must not open a shop."
> —Chinese proverb

It pays to add that smile to your telephone voice, as well. Teleselling experts contend that you have no more than six seconds to make a good impression—or a bad one—on the phone.

Dress For Success

Another quick fix that will help you present yourself better: Dress for success.

To be successful, you have to look the part. You don't have to spend a lot of money on your clothes. But it helps to look as if you did.

For men, that means wearing tailored, natural fiber suits and sport coats, and high-quality silk ties. It means selecting different patterns for your suit, shirt and tie, but a consistent fabric weight.

For women, the "dress for success" look includes natural fabrics, and a single piece of jewelry or a belt that serves as the focal point for your accessories. The accessories you wear, like the briefcase or the leather tote that you carry, should be in proportion to your body size.

Upgrading your appearance is among the most critical of the quick fixes. Others form their first impression of you on the basis of how you look. You never get a second chance to make a good first impression.

Shaking Hands

You may look good but still spoil that initial impression with a limp handshake. Your first marketing maneuver in a face-to-face meeting with a client is to shake hands. Do so with enthusiasm, reaching out your hand and making web-to-web contact with the other person. The "web" between your thumb and first finger should touch theirs.

Another good rule of thumb is that once you've clasped the other hand, match the other person's grip. Continue to be firm only if he or she is, and lighten up if necessary. Some etiquette coaches will even advise you to roll your hand under, giving the other person the upper hand.

Speed Pays

There's a lot to the word "quick." It refers to rapid, low-maintenance, personal-promotion techniques, but it also has to do with a characteristic common to personal promoters. Skilled self-promoters are quick. They hustle.

Top-flight personal salespeople don't just call often, they call early. They're smilin' and dialin' even before their competitors arrive at the office. They attempt to reach decision makers before their offices open—before the gatekeepers arrive. They make all of the day's most important calls by 10 a.m.

The conversations they have are quick and to the point. That goes for their conversations at networking events, or in any other circumstances where they meet prospects. They quickly identify themselves and share

"Off-Hours" Dressing

Most people take care to dress appropriately when they know they will meet a client or prospect. But it's important to dress well whenever you go out in public. If you run into a top prospect at the store, you'll make a poor impression if you're not neatly dressed and groomed. And if you're a service provider like an accountant or insurance agent—you might encounter a new prospect while waiting in a grocery or theater line.

You don't have to be dressed up to be neatly dressed and groomed. Clean and pressed clothing will do the job. Jeans or shorts or other casual clothing can be appropriate depending on the setting. Every time you venture out, consider the possibility that you might bump into your best client.

their commercial. They immediately ask the most important questions, listen for the answers, set up the next step, if necessary, and then move on.

"Quick and to-the-point" also describes the messages they leave and the correspondence they write. They waste no time getting to—or making—their points. They waste no words in communicating their messages in print, or in person.

> "Everything comes to him who hustles while he waits."
> —Thomas Edison

They hustle to obtain the facts they need to conduct business and enhance their expertise. They're quick to get information, and quick to review it.

The best self-promoters hustle to follow up. They're quick to return calls. They're quick to establish the next step with a prospect or client: the next call, the next meeting, the signing of the contract.

And they're quick to send personal notes—via e-mail, regular mail, or any other means—following meetings with prospects, clients, and anyone else they want to influence.

Put Numbers on Your Side

Self-marketers play the numbers game. They know that the more lines they cast, the more fish they'll catch.

Call ten prospects a day. What will that take you, an hour? Just think: 60 minutes a day will enable you to reach out to more than 2,500 prospective buyers in a year. According to estimates, at least 250 of those calls will result in sales.

Check in with at least three clients every day, and ask each for referrals. That will give you over 750 customer contacts a year—considerably more than most of your competitors make.

Invite prospects and clients to lunch or breakfast. Together, those meals provide you with nearly 500 business opportunities a year that you don't get when you dine alone.

Meet ten new people at a monthly networking event, and you'll gain 120 new acquaintances annually.

Finally, give out at least four business cards a day, and you'll distribute 1,000 by the end of the year.

Quick Fixes in Perspective

As you plan to implement these and the other quick-fix ideas, put them in perspective. Understand what these short-term strategies can—and cannot—do for you.

These are simple steps and minor maneuvers, not magical formulas or master plans. Think of them as Band-Aids, rather than cures for your marketing challenges.

> **Spread Your Message**
>
> There are a variety of quick and easy ways to get your name out. Try changing your voice mail message, or laminating and attaching your business card to your luggage, or adding a marketing message to the receipts you distribute.

True, they are shortcuts you can take to gain quick visibility. But they're not keys to gaining long term exposure.

Quick fixes are more likely to save you time than to make you a great deal of money. Yet it's well worth your time to pursue these simple tactics.

Each of these quick hits is an important single step—the kind of step a journey of a million miles begins with.

It's a step that the vast majority of your competitors and other professionals won't take. The more of these steps you take, the more sales you'll make.

Does your success hinge on these quick fixes? No. Your failure to adopt all, or even half of these strategies won't disqualify you in your quest for success.

What matters here is that you take into account your goals, objectives, and challenges as you determine which short-term marketing methods would best suit you.

Persistence Pays

Pay careful attention to the words in "Don't Quit," a poem whose author is unknown:

Success is failure turned inside out —
The silver tint of the clouds of doubt,
And you never can tell how close you are,

> "I am a great believer in luck and the harder I work the more I have of it."
> —Stephen Leacock

It may be near when it seems afar;
So stick to the flight when you're hardest hit,
It's when things seem worst that you mustn't quit."

Author Berton Barkley referred to that same dogged determination this way:

If you want a thing bad enough to go out and fight for it, to give your time, your peace and your sleep for it...if all that you dream and scheme is about it, and life seems useless and worthless without it...if dogged and grim you beseech and beset it, with the help of God, you WILL get it.

Your success will be easier to come by if you promote yourself to others so they believe in you. But you must believe in yourself first.

You must give yourself credit where credit is due. You must understand that you're too good to be your own best kept secret. Once you've sold yourself on yourself, you can sell yourself to others.

Make your personal sale—let yourself and others know how good you are—and you'll achieve a greater level of success and prosperity than you ever dreamed possible.

A Bias for Action

That brings us to the 501st of the ways to "get them to buy from you:" **Go for it.**

You alone must decide what marketing tools "it" represents. Others can and will advise you, but you're the one who must decide on which weapons you want to incorporate into your self-promotion arsenal.

Then you have to use them.

Reading about how to sell yourself is one thing, but doing it is another. Planning to make the personal sale is admirable but meaningless if you don't take action.

Take some action now, even if it amounts to no more than a quick fix or two.

Giving some of the techniques in this book a "try"

isn't good enough, if you are going to achieve much greater success and prosperity.

You need to give these techniques your very best shot—as if your livelihood depended on it. You know what? It does.

Try as you will to make all of these self-promotion strategies work, not all of them will. Accept that. Personal promotion isn't easy; if it were, everyone would do it. But it is critically important.

No doubt you've encountered obstacles along the way, and you will continue to do so. But think of those obstacles as building blocks for success. Heed the words of Tom Watson, the former chairman of IBM: "If you want to succeed, double your failure rate."

> "Success seems to be connected with action. Successful people keep moving. They make mistakes, but they don't quit."
> —Conrad Hilton

Action Ideas and Tips

451 **Communicate with warm smiles and kind words.**
Are there quicker ways to make a positive impression? None come to mind.

Treat others as if they're the most important people on earth. In their minds, they are.

452 **Dial for dollars.** Pick up the phone and start calling. That's still one of the best ways to get business in a short amount of time.

The more calls you make, the more business you'll get. According to one theory, if you call ten people, four will talk to you. Two of those will indicate interest in your product or service, and one will actually buy.

453 **Make one for the road.**
The best thing to do when you've completed your daily quota of calls? Make another call!

Free of the quota pressure with which you began the day, you're likely to come across as more confident and relaxed, and easier to do business with.
—*Power Calling* by Joan Guiducci

454 **Find 'em and phone 'em NOW.** When you're told the boss is "out of the office" or out of town, ask for the phone number to reach him or her immediately. Make the phone connection now and you can save yourself the hassle of leaving messages and playing phone tag.

455 **To make it big, make it early.** Sales trainer Zig ZiglAr reports that 70 percent of all sales are made before 1 p.m., 20 percent between 1 and 4 p.m., and only 10 percent after 4 p.m.

The idea, he says, is to catch prospects when they're most energetic and most responsive.
—*Ziglar on Selling* by Zig ZiglAr

456 **Call and say "hi."** Check in periodically with past and present clients and prospects, even if it's just to find out how they're doing.

It's good customer relations and a nice thing to do. It's also a good way to elicit new orders and repeat business.

457 **Get your name out....**
And, while you're at it, get out your office address, e-mail address, and phone, fax and pager numbers, etc.

If that information is out of clients' and prospects' sight, you'll soon be out of their minds. Include it on everything that you make, print, mail, or distribute; everything! Use labels, business cards and any other form of identification.

Add your Web-page address to your promotional materials, and include it if you offer background information to callers who are on hold.
—*138 Quick Ideas to Get More Clients* by Howard Shenson and Jerry R. Wilson

458 **Schedule power hours.** Block out hours during which you devote full attention to a single revenue-producing activity.

Reserve 8:30–9:30 a.m., for example, as your prospecting hour. Rid yourself of all other distractions during that time, and concentrate only on calling.

Set aside an hour for answering key correspondence and sending out proposals, another hour to connect with clients, etc.

459 **Set tomorrow's priorities today.** Plan ahead for the most important tasks confronting you in the day, week, and month ahead.

Focus on those projects likely to generate the most revenue, and help you achieve your other major goals.

End your day by setting aside time in tomorrow's calendar to accomplish the goals that you deem to be most important.

460 **Use receipts to sell yourself.** Include a commercial on the receipts that you distribute. List your products and services, information about upcoming promotions and sales, details of an award you won, etc.

461 **Laminate your business card.** Display it prominently as an identification tag on your briefcase and luggage.

462 **Buy a badge**. Invest in a heavy duty plastic name badge to use at networking and other professional events. It's sure to make a better impression than those handwritten paper stickers that you pick up as you enter. And if you include a color picture of your product or your brief commercial, your unique name tag can be a conversation starter.

463 **Check it out.** Use company checks to cover local expenses wherever and whenever possible. That goes for lunch, office supplies, car servicing—anything. It provides extra visibility and exposure for your company and yourself.

464 **Get booked.** Your local telephone book is but one of several directories that will carry listings for you and your company. Some others:

- specialized phone books (e.g., those serving seniors or handicapped)
- trade and professional association directories
- chamber of commerce publications
- public library manuals
- city directories
- international directories
- publications of county, state and federal government agencies operating in specialized fields
- computerized electronic "bulletin boards" and data bases

465 **Send a telegram.** Studies show that 93 percent of telegram recipients open them.

Or reach out to your market in other unexpected ways. Enclose your message in a gift, send information by overnight delivery, or do whatever else you can to make your information available in a way that would pique interest and differentiate you from competitors.

466 **Get "listed."** Ask clients, key prospects, and others you seek to influence to be included on their mailing lists.

Ask to be added to their internal as well as outside list. Inside newsletters make you privy to information about purchasing, personnel, priorities, and other topics that can help you in your personal promotion efforts with the organization.

467 **Get "paged."** When you're on the phone with a key prospect, suggest that he or she pull up your Web page.

Your page lends you credibility and establishes your expertise. When others review the page during your call, it supplements their information and enhances your image.

468 **Learn where and when the buck stops.** Discover what you can, as soon as you can, about a prospect's budget. That saves you lots of time down the road.

Find out what the budget is and when it's allocated. Qualify the prospect to determine if they can afford you, and when they'll spend the money. Promoting yourself to a company now may be a time waster if it has already set its budget for the year ahead.

469 **Use "pilot projects" to break the ice.** Reluctant customers

are more likely to do business with you if you propose a "pilot project."

Recommend a short-term trial period in which you provide your services or products. Prospects gain a good introduction to your company without making a future commitment. You gain increased visibility and a foot in the door.

—Jay Conrad Levinson in *Entrepreneur* magazine

470 **Get to know prospects before you meet them.** Gather as much information as you can about prospects prior to your first meeting. Interview staff, go on-line, visit the library and do what ever additional homework you can ahead of time. Do that same kind of research on the participants in a key upcoming meeting.

471 **Show yourself before your stuff.** Communicate your message at a meeting before distributing supporting materials.

Pass out your materials too early, and the focus shifts to them—and away from you.

Grab the attention of your audience and say what you want to say before letting them read what you've written. One exception: those cases where you can't share the information *without* the supporting materials. Then and only then should you distribute the materials ahead of time.

472 **Maximize meetings.** Make the most of each meeting by reviewing the agenda. Focus your attention on, and plan your arrival time around, the most relevant agenda items.

Convene meetings at odd times—say 9:37 a.m. or 4:12 p.m.—to encourage promptness. Or schedule the sessions before lunch or quitting time. That will motivate participants to be brief in their remarks.

Schedule lunch meetings at off hours—say, 11:15 a.m. or 2 p.m.—to avoid the midday rush, and the waiting time that goes with it.
—*SuccessAbilities!* by Paula Ancona

473 **Save the best for last.** Close your business letters with a strong paragraph. Effective final paragraphs include a call for action or a request for the order. Or summarize an argument, make a promise, or seek a rapid response to an important question.

That beats closing with a platitude like "I'm looking forward to hearing from you."
—*Art Sobczak's Telephone Selling Report*

474 **Refine what you say online.** Short is sweet when it comes to online writing.

Use concise information written for a dialogue rather than a monologue. Cut stories into short segments that readers can follow no matter where they jump in.

475 **Seek future commitments.** Suggest your next meeting as the deadline for a prospect to follow through on your recommendations.

Recommend a step that will "move your relationship forward." Ask them to

decide which of your materials most interest them, recommend your proposal to the boss, survey their company's needs, etc.

Getting even a minor commitment will save you lots of time in the future.
—Art Sobczak, writing in the book *Marketing Magic* (editor R. Crandall)

476 **Set deadlines.** Reduce or eliminate waiting time by announcing that you "need this by_____."

Impose deadlines for contract offers to expire, for sources to get back to you with information, for vendors to provide their bid, for job applications, etc.

477 **Let others sweat the small stuff.** Do what you do best, and delegate the rest.

Assign administrative tasks to others in your office, and take on those that generate the most income. If necessary, hire professionals to handle the paperwork and other duties that waste your time.

478 **Pay tribute to timesavers.** Reward staffers who save you time and money.

Offer bonuses, tickets, time off, etc. to those staffers who complete tasks in the shortest amount of time, and free up your time.

479 **Seek outside opinions.** "What would *you* do in my situation?" Pose that question the next time you face challenging circumstances, and helpful advice may come your way.

Even if you don't accept it, the advice may stimulate your thinking.

480 **Help customers help you.** Devise ways to involve customers in developing your business.

Request their help in creating names for new products, services and promotions. Seek their input on other challenges you face in promoting yourself and your organization.

Create a customer advisory board that you consult with regularly.

481 **Feed them and they'll feed you.** Invite your top clients to a customer appreciation breakfast, and get their feedback on your products and services.

Find out what they like best and what they dislike about your services, what would motivate them to buy more often, and how to reach out to more customers like them.

The expense is well worth it. There's no quicker way and probably no better way to conduct market research.

—*The Working Communicator* newsletter

482 **Become more nimble on the Net.** Navigate the Internet more efficiently by creating a Rolodex file of the Net sites you visit most often. To save downloading time, keep a notebook in which you jot down tidbits of information.

—*The Time Management Report* newsletter

483 **Send e-mail messages in bulk.** Transmit information about yourself over e-mail by using the bulk-mail program offered by your Internet service provider. Ask the company how you can send "blind carbon copies," in which only a single address appears on each e-mail message.

Send short messages about your company and yourself, and inform recipients how they can e-mail you back to ask questions, place orders, etc.

484 **Arrange for fast FAXbacks.** Include a return cover sheet with the information you send out by fax. List your name, address and fax number.

That makes it easier for others to respond immediately.

485 **Use old letters in new ways.** Save time on sales correspondence by updating and adapting letters you sent in the past.

Keep a file or computer disc of your response letters. Consult them when others ask questions that were asked before.

Automating your sales letters helps you fine tune them along the way and respond more quickly to inquiries.

486 **Shake the hand that used to feed you.** Offer your products or services to former employers. Or, offer to perform on a part-time basis the kind of full-time services you used to make available. It means extra revenue for you and an opportunity for your former employers to tap into your experience.

487 **Offer something extra.** Come up with a value-added product and service that your competitors don't offer—and offer it.

Ask your best customers to recommend that little something extra, then shop your competitors to make sure they don't make it available.

Possibilities: free maintenance, training classes, an extended warranty, a follow-up consultation.

488 **Deliver the goods now.** Make your products or services available to a new customer immediately. That gets your relationship off to a good start, and lessens the chances the customer will change her mind and call off the deal.

489 **Simplify the sale.** Make it as easy as possible for others to do business with you.

Install a toll-free number. Accept credit cards. Offer a liberal return and exchange policy. Schedule calls, appointments, and deliveries to meet *their* schedules.

490 **Send a note within a day, call within a week.** Follow up on an order with a thank-you note the same day. Don't let a week go by without calling to ask if you can answer any questions or resolve any problems.

491 **Stand behind your service.** Money-back guarantees help turn stalls into sales. They give the message that you believe in what you sell—and sell what you believe in.

492 **Give something away.** It's fast, it's easy, and it's appreciated.

Whether it's a free product or merely an article reprint, your "gift" can open the door to a lasting relationship and future sales.

493 **Let them try before they buy.** Free trials are a quick and easy way to turn contacts into contracts.

Let a prospect try out her product of choice—and provide her with an upgraded, pricier model as well. She may find the higher priced version to be more to her liking, which would be more to yours.

494 **KISS.** Keep It Short and Simple. The point is, *get* to the point. Now! Cut your sales presentation in half. Reduce the verbiage in your marketing materials, on your Web page, on your voice mail.

Keep correspondence to less than one page. Use a few words to communicate ideas for which your competitors need many.

495 **Ask why.** On those occasions when you have to take "no" for an answer, make "why" your question.

Find out why your prospect has chosen not to do business with you. Was price the reason? Your experience? Your reputation?

Listen carefully to the answers, and you'll enhance your chances of closing the deal the next time around.

496 **Stand up.** You resolve problems, and reason more

effectively when you're on your feet.

So say researchers at the University of California. Their studies show an individual processes information up to 20 percent faster when standing up rather than sitting down.

Your most effective "personal salesmanship" comes from an upright position. One reason is that you project and communicate better when you're standing rather than sitting.

—*Sales and Marketing Strategies & News* newsletter

497 **Give yourself the gift of time.** Rise and shine a half hour earlier. Reducing your sack time by just 30 minutes daily gives you an additional 182 1/2 hours of waking time per year. There's a lot of personal promotion you can do with nearly eight additional days in a year.

498 **Eat right, sleep tight.** You'll be more productive by day, and sleep better by night if you follow a sensible diet and exercise regularly.

499 **If it's broke, fix it.** If something isn't working, there's usually a reason.

Give each of your marketing strategies and materials a reasonable time to work, then try something else.

That goes for free publicity campaigns, public speaking programs, networking groups—or any other marketing that you do. If you have to scrap an expensive brochure, redevelop your Web site, fire your publicist—do it. Prepare yourself to change—or expect to be a victim of it.

500 **Refuse to lose.** You'll run into occasional setbacks as you practice the "quick fixes" and all the other self-promotion strategies in this book. That's a given.

But remember that a problem is simply the difference between what you have and what you need. What you need is the commitment to be tough when the going *gets* tough.

501 **Go for it.** You miss 100 percent of the shots you never take. Take one, or better yet many, now. You're too good to be your own best kept secret.

Appendix A

Self-Promotion Success Steps

1 **Take charge.**
Tell yourself to sell yourself.

2 **Take stock.**
Where are you now?

3 **Set goals.**
Where do you want to be?

4 **Get different.**
What makes you special?

5 **Set targets.**
Who needs to know how good you are?

6 **Solve problems.**
Decide what you have that they need.

7 **Scout competitors.**
See what they do, and do it differently.

8 **Seek feedback.**
Get testimonials and referrals from those you've served.

9 **Establish expertise.**
Make a "how to" list.

10 **Create credentials.**
Make a marketing kit.

11 **Take inventory.**
What do your prospects read? What groups do they belong to?

12 **Get published.**
Write and get written about in their publications.

13 **Get booked.**
Get invited to speak to their groups.

14 **Get recognized.**
Spread the word about your accomplishments.

15 **Stay connected.**
Follow up with those who know you — or should.

Appendix B

"Differentiate Yourself" Worksheet

You may *fail* to make the (personal) sale if you can't differentiate yourself from your competitors. Use this worksheet, and the one on the following page, to crystallize in your mind what sets you apart from the rest of the pack.

■ List ten ways you differ from your competitors.

    1.   6.

    2.   7.

    3.   8.

    4.   9.

    5.   10.

■ List your five "onlys"

    1.

    2.

    3.

    4.

    5.

■ List 10 benefits customers get from working with you.

    1.   6.

    2.   7.

    3.   8.

    4.   9.

    5.   10.

■ Write a powerful 50-word commercial. (Consult the Victory Vocabulary list in Chapter 1.)

Appendix C

Self-Promotion Success Principles

1 **You're too good** to be your own best-kept secret.

2 **Sell yourself** on the idea of selling yourself. Recognize the value of recognition.

3 It's good to be good. **It's better if others know about it.**

4 No one else has your ability, background, or skills. **You're one of a kind.** Promote yourself accordingly.

5 **No one can promote you like _you_.** Promote yourself by _yourself._

6 **You are the marketing director** of your own marketing department of your personal corporation.

7 Marketing is smart but **Smart Marketing is smarter.** Smart Marketing means getting maximum impact and exposure for a minimum investment of time and money.

8 **Accept credit where credit is due,** and promote it once you get it.

9 **Create magic in your message** by tuning into the radio station that all those you seek to influence listen to all the time: WMYD (What Makes You Different?).

10 **How you promote yourself is less important** than that you do it differently. Your key to marketing success is to do what your competitors don't.

11 Good things come if you **Make It, Break It, Take It.** Make a plan. Break the news of your accomplishments. Take responsibility for promoting your news.

12 Follow the VCR formula: **Visibility + Creditability = Recognition.** Get that recognition and rewards are sure to follow.

13 "If you done done what you say you done done, then **saying what you done done ain't braggin'.**" (Dizzy Dean)

14 Don't play the Blame Game or the Same Game of marketing. Instead, look in the mirror and say, "**What Is to Be Is Up to Me.**"

15 **Overcome self-doubt and accentuate your positives,** and you'll become an inner winner—and powerful self-promoter.

Appendix D

The Dare-to-Be-Different Checklist

Promote yourself differently, and you'll discover new and different rewards. Follow these guidelines:

- SAY DIFFERENT THINGS ABOUT YOURSELF. Emphasize your "onlys."
- THINK DIFFERENTLY. Focus on today, rather than yesterday or tomorrow.
- ACT DIFFERENTLY. Give the impression that you already are successful.
- SOUND DIFFERENT. Talk the talk of an "arriver," rather than a "striver."
- LOOK DIFFERENT. Develop an appearance that distinguishes you from others.
- SELL YOUR SERVICES DIFFERENTLY. Spell out their unique benefits.
- OFFER SOMETHING DIFFERENT. Make available options that others don't.
- GUARANTEE SOMETHING DIFFERENT. Back up your services in a way that others don't.
- TARGET DIFFERENTLY. Pursue a different niche in the market.
- COMMUNICATE DIFFERENTLY. Get your message across in a unique way.
- FOLLOW UP DIFFERENTLY. Stay in touch in ways to which clients are unaccustomed.

Discover how being different makes a big difference for your business!

About the Author

Fred Berns' "Sell Yourself" message is the centerpiece of the sales and marketing keynote speeches and seminars that he presents worldwide.

His highly-acclaimed presentations for associations, corporations, franchise organizations, and other groups focus on how individuals can use personal promotion to achieve peak sales performance. He has worked with groups as diverse as Johnson & Johnson, the American Automobile Association, the American Society of Interior Designers, the National Pest Control Association, the Environmental Protection Agency, Microsoft, New York Life Insurance, and Mack Trucks.

Berns also consults with and coaches organizations and individuals on how they can differentiate themselves, communicate more effectively, and make a maximum impact for a minimum investment of time and money.

Sell Yourself! 501 Ways to Get Them to Buy from YOU is the latest addition to his "Promotion Power Pack" of books and tapes on sales and marketing.

Berns has received widespread coverage in such media as The Washington Post, National Public Radio, NBC-TV, Newsweek magazine, and national wire services.

A member of the National Speakers Association, Berns launched his speaking and consulting career after working in journalism for 25 years. He founded the Berns Bureau and helped it become one of Washington, DC's largest and longest-established independent news services.

A Chicago native, he now lives with his wife Ellen and son Zachary in Lafayette, Colorado.

How to Contact the Author

For more information about Fred Berns' speaking and consulting services, contact:

Fred Berns
Power Promotion, Inc.
394 Rendezvous Drive
Lafayette, CO 80026

(888) 665-5505
(303) 665-6688
fax: (303) 665-5599
e-mail: FredTalks@aol.com
www.FredBerns.com

Index

ORDER FORM

Sell Yourself!

501 Ways to Get Them to Buy From YOU

☐ **Yes,** send me _____ copies of *Sell Yourself!*
by Fred Berns at $25.00 each.

SHIPPING & HANDLING: $4 for the first item; $2.00 for each additional item.
SALES TAX: Please add $1 per item for each item shipped to Colorado addresses.

☐ Check enclosed

Please charge my: ☐ Visa   ☐ MasterCard   ☐ Amex

CARD NUMBER _____

NAME ON CARD _____ EXP. DATE _____

NAME _____ PHONE_____

COMPANY_____

ADDRESS _____

CITY _____ STATE _____ ZIP_____

✱ Fax orders: 303-665-5599

☎ Phone orders: 888-665-5505 (toll free)

303-665-6688
(Have your Visa, MasterCard, or American Express card ready.)

🖥 Online orders: FredTalks@aol.com / www.FredBerns.com

✉ Mail orders: Fred Berns
Power Promotion, Inc.
394 Rendezvous Dr.
Lafayette, CO 80026

CALL TOLL FREE AND ORDER NOW

Berns' Business Builders

Marketing materials that will bring you recognition and rewards

CELEBRATE MARKETING *(book)*
An anthology on networking, on-line marketing, referrals and more. Includes a disk with tips from some of America's best marketing minds.

151 SELL-YOURSELF IDEAS *(manual)*
A "hands on" marketing resource that provides insights on gaining visibility, credibility and rewards.

DARE TO BE DIFFERENT SELF PROMOTION *(booklet)*
The publication that focuses on promoting your uniqueness, and marketing yourself differently.

CONFESSIONS OF SHAMELESS SELF PROMOTERS *(book)*
Strategies, secrets, shortcuts and stories from 68 self promotion gurus. Great self marketing tips on technology, pricing, branding and more.

SELF PROMOTION NEWS & VIEWS *(special report)*
A unique collection of articles on what's hot and what's not, do's and don'ts, and tips and trends in personal marketing today.

VICTORY VOCABULARY
A laminated list of 75 winning words that professionals should choose to use in their marketing messages and materials.

EASY TO ORDER . . .

✱ Fax orders: 303-665-5599

☎ Phone orders: 888-665-5505 (toll free)
　　　　　　　　303-665-6688

▇ Online orders: FredTalks@aol.com/
　　　　www.FredBerns.com

✉ Mail orders:
　　　Fred Berns
　　　Power Promotion, Inc.
　　　394 Rendezvous Dr.
　　　Lafayette, CO 80026

	Price	*Qty.*	*Amount*
Celebrate Marketing book	$25		
News & Views report	$25		
Confessions book	$20		
151 Ideas manual	$15		
Dare To Be Different booklet	$15		
Victory Vocabulary card	$10		
Power Pack of all 6	$100		
Subtotal			
Shipping & Handling			$6
TOTAL			

☐ Check enclosed　–or–　Please charge my: ☐ Visa　☐ MasterCard　☐ Amex

CARD NUMBER_____

NAME ON CARD _____ EXP. DATE_____

NAME _____ PHONE_____

COMPANY_____

ADDRESS _____

CITY _____ STATE _____ ZIP_____

Call toll free and order now